EVERYTHING HAS ITS TIME

Ecclesiastes

N E L S O N
I M P A C T™
Bible Study Series

EVERYTHING
HAS ITS TIME

Ecclesiastes

NELSON IMPACT
A Division of Thomas Nelson Publishers
Since 1798

www.thomasnelson.com

The publishers are grateful to Michael Christopher for his collaboration, writing skills, and editorial help in developing the content for this book.

Published by Nelson Impact, a division of Thomas Nelson, Inc., P.O. Box 141000, Nashville, Tennessee 37214.

ISBN: 1-4185-0865-9

Printed in the United States of America.

07 08 EB 9 8 7 6 5 4 3 2

A Word from the Publisher...

*Be diligent to present yourself approved to God, a worker who does not need
to be ashamed, rightly dividing the word of truth.*

2 Timothy 2:15 NKJV

We are so glad that you have chosen this study guide to enrich your biblical knowledge and strengthen your walk with God. Inside you will find great information that will deepen your understanding and knowledge of this book of the Bible.

Many tools are included to aid you in your study, including ancient and present-day maps of the Middle East, as well as timelines and charts to help you understand when the book was written and why. You will also benefit from sidebars placed strategically throughout this study guide, designed to give you expanded knowledge of language, theology, culture, and other details regarding the Scripture being studied.

We consider it a joy and a ministry to serve you and teach you through these study guides. May your heart be blessed, your mind expanded, and your spirit lifted as you walk through God's Word.

Blessings,

Edward (Les) Middleton, M.Div.
Associate Publisher, Nelson Impact

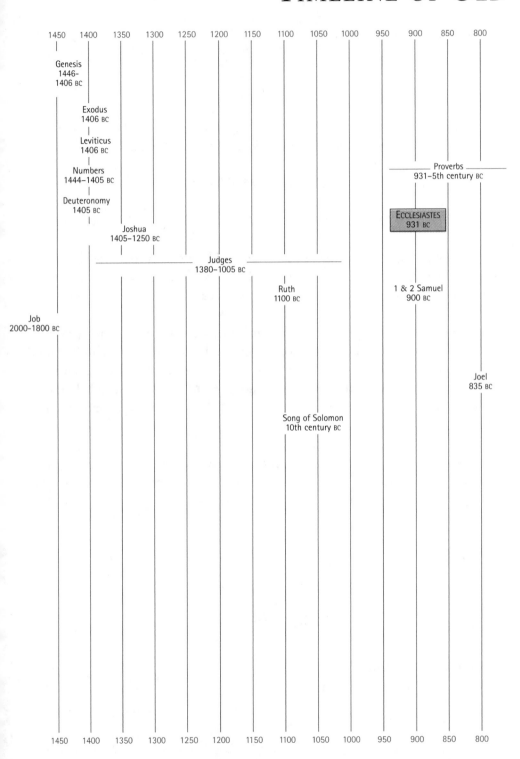

| 1450 | 1400 | 1350 | 1300 | 1250 | 1200 | 1150 | 1100 | 1050 | 1000 | 950 | 900 | 850 | 800 |

Genesis
1446–
1406 BC

Exodus
1406 BC

Leviticus
1406 BC

Numbers
1444–1405 BC

Proverbs
931–5th century BC

Deuteronomy
1405 BC

ECCLESIASTES
931 BC

Joshua
1405–1250 BC

Judges
1380–1005 BC

Ruth
1100 BC

1 & 2 Samuel
900 BC

Job
2000–1800 BC

Joel
835 BC

Song of Solomon
10th century BC

| 1450 | 1400 | 1350 | 1300 | 1250 | 1200 | 1150 | 1100 | 1050 | 1000 | 950 | 900 | 850 | 800 |

TESTAMENT WRITINGS

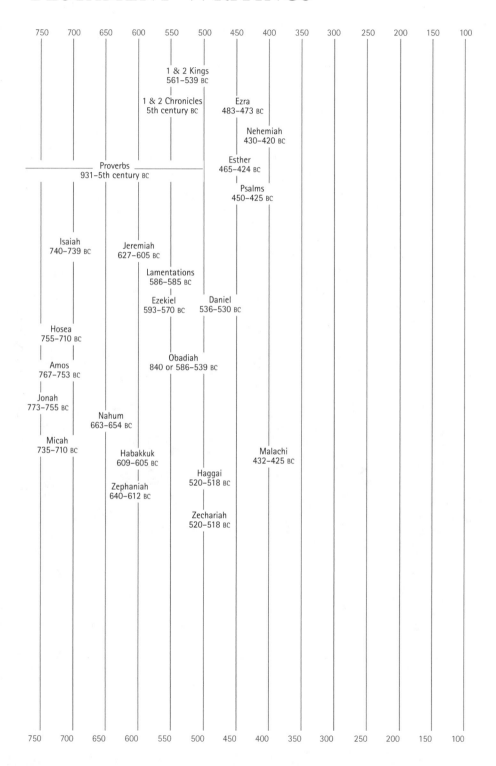

750 700 650 600 550 500 450 400 350 300 250 200 150 100

1 & 2 Kings
561–539 BC

1 & 2 Chronicles
5th century BC

Ezra
483–473 BC

Nehemiah
430–420 BC

Proverbs
931–5th century BC

Esther
465–424 BC

Psalms
450–425 BC

Isaiah
740–739 BC

Jeremiah
627–605 BC

Lamentations
586–585 BC

Ezekiel
593–570 BC

Daniel
536–530 BC

Hosea
755–710 BC

Obadiah
840 or 586–539 BC

Amos
767–753 BC

Jonah
773–755 BC

Nahum
663–654 BC

Micah
735–710 BC

Habakkuk
609–605 BC

Malachi
432–425 BC

Haggai
520–518 BC

Zephaniah
640–612 BC

Zechariah
520–518 BC

750 700 650 600 550 500 450 400 350 300 250 200 150 100

OLD MIDDLE EAST

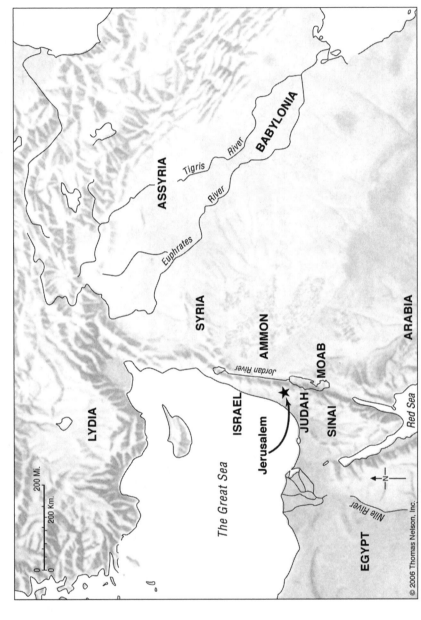

★ Scholars believe that the book of Ecclesiastes was written in Jerusalem, where Solomon lived most of his life.

MIDDLE EAST OF TODAY

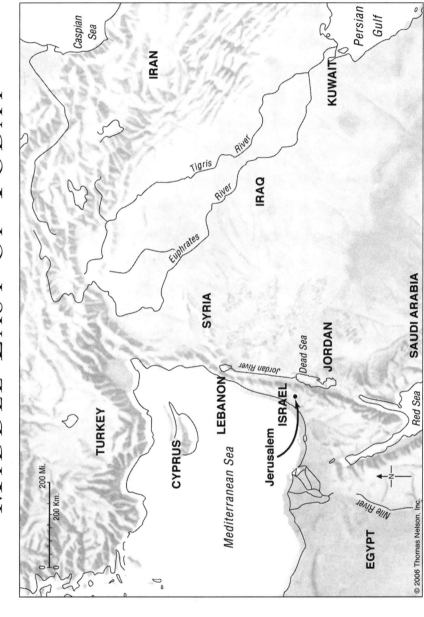

OLD TESTAMENT DIVISIONS

The Pentateuch
Genesis
Exodus
Leviticus
Numbers
Deuteronomy

Wisdom Literature
Job
Psalms
Proverbs
Ecclesiastes
Song of Solomon

The Historical Books
Joshua
Judges
Ruth
1 Samuel
2 Samuel
1 Kings
2 Kings
1 Chronicles
2 Chronicles
Ezra
Nehemiah
Esther

The Prophetic Books
Isaiah
Jeremiah
Lamentations
Ezekiel
Daniel
Hosea
Joel
Amos
Obadiah
Jonah
Micah
Nahum
Habakkuk
Zephaniah
Haggai
Zechariah
Malachi

New Testament Divisions

The Four Gospels
Matthew
Mark
Luke
John

History
Acts

The Epistles of Paul
Romans
1 Corinthians
2 Corinthians
Galatians
Ephesians
Philippians
Colossians
1 Thessalonians
2 Thessalonians
1 Timothy
2 Timothy
Titus
Philemon

The General Epistles
Hebrews
James
1 Peter
2 Peter
1 John
2 John
3 John
Jude

Apocalyptic Literature
Revelation

ICON KEY

Throughout this study guide, you will find many icon sidebars that will aid and enrich your study of this book of the Bible. To help you identify what these icons represent, please refer to the key below.

BIBLICAL GRAB BAG

A biblical grab bag full of interesting facts and tidbits.

BIBLE

Further exploration of biblical principles and interpretations, along with a little food for thought.

LANGUAGE

Word usages, definitions, interpretations, and information on the Greek and Hebrew languages.

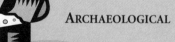
CULTURE

Customs, traditions, and lifestyle practices in biblical times.

ARCHAEOLOGICAL

Archaeological discoveries and artifacts that relate to biblical life, as well as modern-day discoveries.

CONTENTS

INTRODUCTION

Take a good look at the following quotations. Then ask yourself how many of these you would automatically recognize as extracts from the book of Ecclesiastes, if you came across them anywhere except in a study guide to that same book.

- "Vanity of vanities, all is vanity" (Eccl. 1:2).
- "The sun also rises . . ." (Eccl. 1:5).
- "To everything there is a season . . ." (Eccl. 3:1).
- "Two are better than one . . ." (Eccl. 4:9).
- "A good name is better than precious ointment" (Eccl. 7:1).
- "The race is not to the swift, nor the battle to the strong, nor bread to the wise, nor riches to men of understanding, nor favor to men of skill; but time and chance happen to them all" (Eccl. 9:11).
- "Cast your bread upon the waters, for you will find it after many days" (Eccl. 11:1).
- "Remember now your Creator in the days of your youth" (Eccl. 12:1).
- "Much study is wearisome to the flesh" (Eccl. 12:12).
- "Let us hear the conclusion of the whole matter: Fear God and keep His commandments, for this is man's all" (Eccl. 12:13).

Now ask yourself another question. Assuming you have a basic familiarity with Ecclesiastes—meaning that you've read parts of it or heard parts of it read or talked about or quoted—what is your impression? Is the overall tone of Ecclesiastes positive or negative? What about its message?

These are a few of the things we will examine as we work through Ecclesiastes together. But first, let's deal with some of the who, what, where, and when questions that could have a lot of bearing on how you will eventually assess its true value, and its relevance to your own life.

WHAT'S IN A NAME?

The name *Ekklēsiastēs* comes from the Septuagint. The Septuagint is the well-known translation of the Hebrew Scriptures into Greek on which many modern translations are based. It was produced by a team of about seventy highly qualified Hebrew scholars (*septuaginta* is Latin for "seventy") sometime in the years between 300 and 200 BC.

Ekklēsiastēs means "one who calls an assembly." Obviously, we get the modern English word *Ecclesiastes* from the same Greek word.

WAS SOLOMON REALLY THE AUTHOR?

To many people, the question of Solomon's authorship might seem a little out of place. Why would anyone doubt that David's son, King Solomon, wrote the book of Ecclesiastes? Isn't his authorship of the book a long-established fact?

In truth, it's more of a "long-accepted likelihood," which isn't quite the same thing. There is absolutely nothing within the book itself that tells us who wrote it for sure. Granted, the author calls himself "the Preacher, the son of David, king in Jerusalem" in the very first verse, but David had more than one son. In fact, 1 Chronicles 3:1–8 lists nineteen sons of David, all born to his various wives. But verse 9 also tells us that these do not include any sons born to concubines, so the pool of potential authors—at least in theory—could be even bigger.

On the other hand, the author himself tells us that he had "attained greatness" and "gained more wisdom than all who were before me in Jerusalem" (Eccl. 1:16). He also tells us that he built a number of houses, vineyards, gardens, orchards, and

The Sons of David

Even though most scholars believe Solomon was the author of Ecclesiastes, the author's reference to himself as a "son of David" is not by itself a very defining comment! Here are the names of nineteen sons of David that we know about for sure.* These do not include additional children born to various concubines.

Born in Hebron . . .
(1) Amnon, by Ahinoam the Jezreelitess;
(2) Daniel, by Abigail the Carmelitess;
(3) Absalom the son of Maacah, the daughter of Talmai, king of Geshur;
(4) Adonijah the son of Haggith;
(5) Shephatiah, by Abital; and
(6) Ithream, by Eglah.

Born in Jerusalem . . .
(7) Shimea, (8) Shobab, (9) Nathan, and (10) Solomon, by Bathsheba, the daughter of Ammiel; and
(11) Ibhar, (12) Elishama, (13) Eliphelet, (14) Nogah, (15) Nepheg, (16) Japhia, (17) Elishama, (18) Eliada, and (19) Eliphelet, by various other wives.

*Note that these names come from 1 Chronicles 19:1–10. Some are spelled differently in other places in the Bible.

even water pools (2:4–6); that he acquired many servants (2:7); and that he owned a great deal of silver and gold, supported many male and female singers, and had "musical instruments of all kinds" (2:8).

Clearly the author of Ecclesiastes was no ordinary man. Indeed, he tells us, "I became great and excelled more than all who were before me in Jerusalem. Also my wisdom remained with me" (Eccl. 2:9 NKJV). He certainly sounds like Solomon.

Meanwhile, scholars who deny Solomon's authorship point to what were once considered "later" stylistic and word-choice issues. They argue that some Hebrew words and idioms that are in the original text—and even some Persian words as well—simply were not being used in Solomon's era.

On the other hand, dating ancient texts by word studies alone can be a difficult, sometimes frustrating job, even on a good day. As with any other science, new discoveries often make old ones obsolete. More than one long-held assumption about the age of an ancient text has been proven false by new evidence.

Probably the single best-known modern discovery, which forced scholars to rethink many prior assumptions, is the discovery of the Dead Sea Scrolls in the mid-twentieth century. Several assumptions about the antiquity of certain words and expressions that had seemed fairly significant turned out to be false. In fact, some words were far more ancient than many scholars had once believed, which helped resolve the authorship question in the case of Ecclesiastes—at least for some.

In terms of an actual date for Ecclesiastes, Solomon probably died somewhere around 930 BC. It seems reasonable to assume that he would have written this book nearer the end of his life than the beginning, based on the life experiences it reveals. That might put it sometime after 960 or 950 BC.

But Why So Negative?

The *why* of Ecclesiastes is a much bigger question. If we could do a scientific poll and ask one thousand people who were introduced to Ecclesiastes in Sunday school—and who also have read it as adults—it's quite possible that a majority would see Ecclesiastes in a negative light. "All is vanity, so nothing is worth doing" seems like the major theme, as shown in the table titled "The Nine Major Vanities of Solomon" on page 5 of this study guide.

To be more precise, maybe we should say that Solomon seems to be grouping all the potential failures of humankind into three major categories: failures of (1) works, (2) wisdom, and (3) righteousness. Thus, no matter how much work you do to

THE NINE MAJOR VANITIES OF SOLOMON

Specific Vanity	Solomon's Comments*
Toil	I have seen all the works that are done under the sun; and indeed, all is vanity and grasping for the wind. (1:14) Then I looked on all the works that my hands had done And on the labor in which I had toiled; And indeed all was vanity and grasping for the wind. There was no profit under the sun. (2:11)
Pleasure	I said in my heart, "Come now, I will test you with mirth; therefore enjoy pleasure"; but surely, this also was vanity. I said of laughter—"Madness!"; and of mirth, "What does it accomplish?" (2:1–2)
Wisdom	So I said in my heart, "As it happens to the fool, It also happens to me, And why was I then more wise?" Then I said in my heart, "This also is vanity." (2:15)
Wealth	For God gives wisdom and knowledge and joy to a man who is good in His sight; but to the sinner He gives the work of gathering and collecting, that he may give to him who is good before God. This also is vanity and grasping for the wind. (2:26)
Power and Prestige	There was no end of all the people over whom he was made king; Yet those who come afterward will not rejoice in him. Surely this also is vanity and grasping for the wind. (4:16)
Life Itself	For who knows what is good for man in life, all the days of his vain life which he passes like a shadow? Who can tell a man what will happen after him under the sun? (6:12)
Righteousness	There is a vanity which occurs on earth, that there are just men to whom it happens according to the work of the wicked; again, there are wicked men to whom it happens according to the work of the righteous. I said that this also is vanity. (8:14)
After Death	But if a man lives many years And rejoices in them all, Yet let him remember the days of darkness, For they will be many. All that is coming is vanity. (11:8)
Childhood and Youth	Therefore remove sorrow from your heart, And put away evil from your flesh, For childhood and youth are vanity. (11:10)

*All quotations in this table are taken from the *New King James Version* of the Bible.

acquire possessions and wealth, all these things can be swept away in a moment. Or no matter how much education and wisdom you acquire, you can never be sure that wisdom alone will make your life easier. A little sin, a little sickness, a little bad timing, and the fruit of wisdom can be taken away in a flash.

Even righteousness gives us no guarantees. How often do we see the righteous person punished and the wicked person win—at least in modern courtrooms?

And yet the question we really have to answer is, what was Solomon's own position on all this? Solomon was the wisest man who ever lived, so what was the real fruit of his wisdom? Was he merely giving a critique of modern secular humanism (see definition below) three thousand years before it took over much of our modern culture—or did he have something else in mind?

SAY THAT AGAIN?

Secular humanism is a fairly modern worldview in which man himself becomes the measure of all things. The eternal values taught in the Bible simply do not exist; things are good because someone says they are good, or bad because someone says they are bad. Thus, there are no absolutes, only "relative values" that ride on the tides of public opinion.

This "something else" is the true essence of the book of Ecclesiastes. In a sense it's a little like a mystery that you have to read *all the way through* to know how it turns out. You can't break Ecclesiastes into little pieces and think you have the whole message. It's fine to extract smaller truths here and there, but as with so much of the Bible, a "bits and pieces" approach doesn't work very well.

What was Solomon really saying? What was his true message? Did he believe that anything at all was worth trying, worth doing, worth being? In what—or whom—did the wisest man of all time truly trust?

Let's read on and find out.

esu WHO IS "THE PREACHER"?

The Hebrew word in verse 1 that refers to the author of Ecclesiastes and is most often translated "preacher" or "teacher" is accompanied by what English grammarians call the article "the" in the original text. This is what suggests that "the Preacher" is a title rather than a name. Unfortunately, this particular word is used to refer to no one else in the Old Testament, so its exact meaning is difficult to establish.

The Hebrew word itself is often transliterated into English as *Qōhelet* (or *qohelet*) and is sometimes treated as an actual name, but most scholars believe—as indicated above—that it is really a title. That's where they get the concept of "teacher" or "preacher," meaning one who attempts to impart wisdom and knowledge to an "assembly."

1

ALL IS VANITY
UNDER THE SUN

ECCLESIASTES 1

Before We Begin . . .

Before you begin to study Ecclesiastes, what one word (or group of words) can you think of that occurs most often within its pages? In other words, what have you already heard about this book?

Ecclesiastes is an example of Jewish wisdom literature. Can you name any other examples of wisdom literature in the Bible?

The first verse of Ecclesiastes identifies its author as a "son of David." By itself, this verse is not very convincing, but taken together with some of the other verses we examined in the introduction to this study guide (especially 1:12), the overall body of evidence certainly suggests that we are reading the words of Solomon. We therefore will refer to Solomon as the author from this point forward.

ECCLESIASTES 1

THE VANITY OF LIFE

The word "Preacher" in verse 1 is given as "Teacher" in some other translations of the Bible. Keep this in mind as you read through the text so that you can decide for yourself which word is a better fit. Is the author teaching or preaching? Or both?

Please read the first chapter of Ecclesiastes and respond to the following questions.

What is the word Solomon uses in verse 2 to establish his theme for the rest of the book?

How would you define this word in a modern context? What do you think Solomon means by it?

Do you think Solomon is referring specifically to those who labor outdoors, such as highway workers and farmers, when he speaks of toiling "under the sun" (v. 3)? If not, what do you think he means?

What is the contrast Solomon sets up between verses 2–4a and verses 4b–7? Works of [what] versus works of [what]?

For extra credit, what famous American author wrote a book with a title based on verse 5? What is that title?

What does the wind do (v. 6)? Does the author mean to imply that wind has a regular "circuit" that it travels every day?

What do you think Solomon means when he talks about the rivers returning to "the place from which [they came]" (v. 7)? Did Solomon believe that rivers could reverse their direction?

How would you restate verse 9 in simpler terms? What is Solomon saying here?

Verse 11 makes a statement that has been repeated many times down through the centuries. One of the most memorable restatements, not necessarily anchored to this verse by its author but still cited many times by those commenting on current events, was uttered by George Santayana: "Those who cannot remember the past are condemned to repeat it."

What would be your own restatement of this timeless principle?

THE GRIEF OF WISDOM

In the first eleven verses of chapter 1, Solomon laid out what his main theme would be through much of Ecclesiastes—*the futility of human effort to achieve anything worthwhile and lasting.* Starting in verse 12, he now begins to make his case from four different perspectives, shown in the chart below.

Perspective	Reference
Human achievement	1:12–15
Human wisdom	1:16–18; 2:12–17
Pleasure seeking	2:1–11
Toil or labor	2:18–6:9

WHAT IS THE WISDOM LITERATURE?

Both ancient and modern Jews organize the books of the Bible into three groups: the Law (*Torah*), the Prophets (*Nevi'im*), and the Writings (*Ketuvim*). From the first letters of these three words, they extract an acronym, which might be spelled phonetically as *TaNaK* and became *Tanakh* in most modern spellings. Thus, *Tanakh* is the Jewish word for "Bible."

The last of the three groups of books (the Writings) contains three examples of what is also called the Wisdom Literature by both Jews and Christians. These include Job, Proverbs, and Ecclesiastes. Song of Solomon is sometimes included in this group, but not by everyone. Other books (especially Psalms) contain plenty of human wisdom, but the Wisdom Literature itself is unique in the following ways:

1. The Wisdom Literature bases any claim it might have to authority on *tradition* and *observation*. It doesn't claim to be speaking for God or even interpreting His Word. Rather, it deals with things that other people can observe for themselves if they look. Most often it is based on fundamental social structures, such as the family.

2. The Wisdom Literature focuses on everyday life, especially on how to live productively, comfortably, and well. It tends to focus on the "big" issues that all people have to face every day. It also focuses on personal relationships between people; it doesn't deal much with history, politics, or religious issues. Basically it deals with harmony and order between people and between people and God.

3. The Wisdom Literature does not appeal to (or pretend to represent) "revealed truth." It deals with things from a human perspective—with what people can do on their own to address their own condition. It focuses on what we often call the "real world" and attempts to find the best possible course of action for most of life's situations.

4. The Wisdom Literature evolves out of reverence for, and commitment to, God. It starts with the fundamental assumption that the God of the Israelites is the one true creator of the universe. It therefore studies the universe to learn more about God, especially about His character and His sense of order—and about how to live in harmony with Him.

What does Solomon say in verse 12 that helps confirm that he was indeed the author of Ecclesiastes? How many others, who were also sons of David, could make the same claim?

What does he say he set his heart to do (v. 13)?

What theme does Solomon return to in verses 14–15?

What two things does he say cannot be "fixed" (v. 15)?

WHEN IS VANITY NOT VANITY?

It's worth noting that some translations of the Bible do not use the word "vanity" in Ecclesiastes 1:2. For example, the New Living Translation and the New International Version use the word "meaningless," while the *Amplified Bible* uses "vapor of vapors" and "futility." *The Message* even uses the word "smoke," as in "It's all smoke."

The original Hebrew word was *hebel*, perhaps most accurately translated "meaningless" even though "vanity" has probably become better known, having been around since it was introduced in the King James Version near the beginning of the seventeenth century.

In verse 16, Solomon provides even more information about himself, saying, "Look, I have attained greatness, and have gained more wisdom than all who were before me in Jerusalem. My heart has understood great wisdom and knowledge" (NKJV).

What did Solomon set his heart to know (v. 17)?

Do you agree with the "wisdom" expressed in verse 18? Why or why not? What qualifying statements might you want to add to Solomon's own words?

PULLING IT ALL TOGETHER . . .

• Solomon begins Ecclesiastes by identifying himself as a son of David. But David had many sons, so this is not exactly a definitive qualification!

• Solomon then introduces his main theme, that all of man's striving—by itself—is meaningless vanity.

• Next, he sets up a contrast between the efforts of man and the timeless independence of events in the natural realm. No matter what man does, he cannot have influence on the sun or the earth, nor the winds or the rivers.

• Finally, he begins illustrating his main theme from personal experience and says that so-called wisdom simply leads to sorrow and grief.

VANITY OF PLEASURE, PRESTIGE, AND AFFLUENCE

ECCLESIASTES 2

Before We Begin . . .

Based on your personal experience, do you believe that pleasure, prestige, and affluence automatically lead to moral and spiritual emptiness, or meaninglessness? (This latter word might be closer to what Solomon means by the word "vanity.")

What do you think will be Solomon's answer to the question above?

ECCLESIASTES 2

THE VANITY OF PLEASURE

Ecclesiastes 2 deals with an experiment Solomon conducted in regard to the value of human achievement. According to verse 1, what did he "test" with, and what did he "therefore enjoy" as much as he was able?

What word did he use to describe laughter—presumably his own (v. 2)?

What did he say about mirth? That is, what question did he ask?

Fill in the blanks in the verse below, then read it carefully to determine whether Solomon's experiment—as laid out above—was truly scientific.

> *I searched in my heart how to gratify my flesh with* pleasure *, while guiding my heart with* wisdom*, and how to lay hold on* folly *, till I might see what was good for the sons of men to do under* heaven *all the days of their lives. (Eccl. 2:3 NKJV)*

What is your verdict—do you think Solomon was objective? Why or why not?

In verses 4–8, Solomon lists a number of his accomplishments. Compared to other lists of Solomon's possessions in the Bible (see the sidebar "How Wise and How Rich Was Solomon Anyway?" elsewhere in this chapter), this passage isn't especially impressive, but it does help to identify him. Besides, he really wasn't intending to brag here; it seems more likely that he was simply trying to establish his credentials as one who had done much, owned much, and been in charge of much—and therefore knew what he was talking about.

Read this short passage, then list a few of the things Solomon takes credit for in the space provided.

> *I made my works great, I built myself houses, and planted myself vineyards. I made myself gardens and orchards, and I planted all kinds of fruit trees in them. I*

*made myself water pools from which to water the grow-
ing trees of the grove. I acquired male and female servants, and had servants born in my house. Yes, I had
greater possessions of herds and flocks than all who were
in Jerusalem before me. I also gathered for myself silver
and gold and the special treasures of kings and of the
provinces. I acquired male and female singers, the
delights of the sons of men, and musical instruments of
all kinds. (Eccl. 2:4–8 NKJV)*

According to the above verses, what did Solomon make or build?

What did he plant?

What did he acquire, or own?

*Moving on, in verse 9 Solomon claims, "I became great and
excelled more than all who were before me in Jerusalem." What
also "remained with" him?*

*Does this last statement in verse 9 tend to make him more or less
believable? Why?*

How Wise and How Rich Was Solomon Anyway?

In 1 Kings 10:14 we are told that "the weight of gold that came to Solomon yearly was six hundred and sixty-six talents of gold." This translates to about 600,000 troy ounces. At a modern price of about $500 an ounce, that much gold would work out to an annual income of about $300 million in today's currency. In addition, some scholars estimate that Solomon may have been presented with as much as $25 billion in gold by his father, David, for the construction of the temple.

But this was really only the beginning. In fact, it is impossible to appreciate the wisdom and riches of Solomon without reading what the Bible itself tells us in the following two excerpts from 1 Kings. Please take the time to read these two passages, for two very good reasons: (1) they truly establish the extent of Solomon's wisdom, on which so much of the book of Ecclesiastes is built; and (2) they also establish the extent of his riches even as they give us some idea of the "life experience" he must have had to own and manage all these things.

Here is what the Bible says about Solomon's wisdom and riches:

Solomon reigned over all kingdoms from the River to the land of the Philistines, as far as the border of Egypt. They brought tribute and served Solomon all the days of his life. Now Solomon's provision for one day was thirty kors of fine flour, sixty kors of meal, ten fatted oxen, twenty oxen from the pastures, and one hundred sheep, besides deer, gazelles, roebucks, and fatted fowl. For he had dominion over all the region on this side of the River from Tiphsah even to Gaza, namely over all the kings on this side of the River; and he had peace on every side all around him. And Judah and Israel dwelt safely, each man under his vine and his fig tree, from Dan as far as Beersheba, all the days of Solomon.

Solomon had forty thousand stalls of horses for his chariots, and twelve thousand horsemen. And these governors, each man in his month, provided food for King Solomon and for all who came to King Solomon's table. There was no lack in their supply. They also brought barley and straw to the proper place, for the horses and steeds, each man according to his charge.

And God gave Solomon wisdom and exceedingly great understanding, and largeness of heart like the sand on the seashore. Thus Solomon's wisdom excelled the wisdom of all the men of the East and all the wisdom of Egypt. For he was wiser than all men . . . and his fame was in all the surrounding nations. He spoke three thousand proverbs, and his songs were one thousand

and five. Also he spoke of trees, from the cedar tree of Lebanon even to the hyssop that springs out of the wall; he spoke also of animals, of birds, of creeping things, and of fish. And men of all nations, from all the kings of the earth who had heard of his wisdom, came to hear the wisdom of Solomon. (1 Kin. 4:21–34 NKJV)

The weight of gold that came to Solomon yearly was six hundred and sixty-six talents of gold, besides that from the traveling merchants, from the income of traders, from all the kings of Arabia, and from the governors of the country.

And King Solomon made two hundred large shields of hammered gold; six hundred shekels of gold went into each shield. He also made three hundred shields of hammered gold; three minas of gold went into each shield. . . .

Moreover the king made a great throne of ivory, and overlaid it with pure gold. The throne had six steps, and the top of the throne was round at the back; there were armrests on either side of the place of the seat, and two lions stood beside the armrests. Twelve lions stood there, one on each side of the six steps; nothing like this had been made for any other kingdom.

All King Solomon's drinking vessels were gold, and all the vessels of the House of the Forest of Lebanon were pure gold. Not one was silver, for this was accounted as nothing in the days of Solomon. For the king had merchant ships at sea with the fleet of Hiram. Once every three years the merchant ships came bringing gold, silver, ivory, apes, and monkeys. So King Solomon surpassed all the kings of the earth in riches and wisdom.

Now all the earth sought the presence of Solomon to hear his wisdom, which God had put in his heart. Each man brought his present: articles of silver and gold, garments, armor, spices, horses, and mules, at a set rate year by year.

And Solomon gathered chariots and horsemen; he had one thousand four hundred chariots and twelve thousand horsemen, whom he stationed in the chariot cities and with the king at Jerusalem. The king made silver as common in Jerusalem as stones, and he made cedar trees as abundant as the sycamores which are in the lowland.

Also Solomon had horses imported from Egypt and Keveh; the king's merchants bought them in Keveh at the current price. Now a chariot that was imported from Egypt cost six hundred shekels of silver, and a horse one hundred and fifty; and thus, through their agents, they exported them to all the kings of the Hittites and the kings of Syria. (1 Kin. 10:14–29 NKJV)

Read verses 10–11, one at a time, and notice the direct cause-effect relationship between the two:

> Whatever my eyes desired I did not keep from them.
> I did not withhold my heart from any pleasure,
> For my heart rejoiced in all my labor;
> And this was my reward from all my labor.
>
> Then I looked on all the works that my hands had done
> And on the labor in which I had toiled;
> And indeed all was vanity and grasping for the wind.
> There was no profit under the sun. (NKJV)

Do these seem to you like the words and conclusions of a man who has done his homework, as we might say today, or (to borrow another modern expression) is he just talking through his hat? Why?

THE END OF THE WISE AND THE FOOLISH

In verse 12, Solomon makes it clear that his accomplishments might be duplicated, but they could not be bettered by anyone else—at least, not in his own time and place. What does he then say about wisdom versus folly (v. 13)? Does he still prefer one over the other?

What does he say the fool does (v. 14)?

Even so, what is this "same event" he mentions in the last half of verse 14, which "happens to them all"? He speaks of "it" again in the first half of verse 15. What is he talking about?

What is his conclusion? To what does the word "this" refer in the last sentence of verse 15?

Verse 16 sums up everything Solomon has said in the four preceding verses. Fill in the blanks below to see his conclusion.

> *For there is no more ~~remembered~~ of the wise than of*
> *the fool forever,*
> *Since all that now is will be ~~forgotten~~ in the days*
> *to come.*
> *And how does a wise man die?*
> *As the fool!*
> *(Eccl. 2:16 NKJV)*

Solomon expands on the above in the next few verses. For example, what does he say he hated (v. 17)? life

Why does he say he hated it?

meaningless

What does he say he hated in verse 18?

all the things for which he toiled for under the sun

Again, why does he say he hated it? Do these sound like the words of a greedy, ungenerous man, or is something else going on here?

What is the conundrum (i.e., the problem with no clear solution) to which Solomon alludes in verse 19? Why would this trouble him?

Again, what is his conclusion at the end of verse 19?

Pay special attention now to the shift in Solomon's emphasis, from "I" or "my" in verse 18 (and the preceding verses as well) to "he," "a man," and "his," beginning in verse 19 and shown even more clearly in verses 20–21. In verse 20 he talks again about himself; in verse 21 he makes the switch, which he then continues for several more chapters, at least until verse 9 of chapter 6.

This is how Solomon generalized his experiences and the conclusions he drew from them, from those that were personal and private to those that—at least in his own mind—were universal and could be applied to everyone. But if you miss the switch, it's hard to keep track of what's going on!

In general, verses 20–23 expand on what Solomon has already said. For example, in verse 20 he says he "turned [his] heart." In modern English, what does this mean?

Again, in verse 21, Solomon speaks of leaving his heritage to someone who has not earned it. Do you think this is a common sentiment in the present age? What might parents do nowadays to avoid this kind of feeling in their old age—assuming they've had reasonable success in life?

In verse 22, it's important to get the emphasis right in order to get the meaning right. The word "has" must be emphasized, meaning "What does a man *retain* as a reward for all his labor?"

Verse 23 includes one of the few references in the Bible to what we tend to think of as a modern condition only, usually arising from too much work and too much worry. What is that reference, and how does it translate into modern English?

To conclude Ecclesiastes 2, please read verses 24–26, reprinted below, and respond to the question that follows.

> *Nothing is better for a man than that he should eat and drink, and that his soul should enjoy good in his labor. This also, I saw, was from the hand of God. For who can eat, or who can have enjoyment, more than I? For God gives wisdom and knowledge and joy to a man who is good in His sight; but to the sinner He gives the work of gathering and collecting, that he may give to him who is*

good before God. This also is vanity and grasping for the wind. (NKJV)

What is Solomon's conclusion, taken from his discussion of his own wisdom and possessions? In the end, what does he say he really values, and where does it come from?

PULLING IT ALL TOGETHER . . .

• Solomon begins chapter 2 of Ecclesiastes by conducting an experiment in regard to what he saw as the value of human achievement.

• He then lists a few of his achievements; he admits that others might duplicate them but claims that no one can exceed them.

• Then Solomon admits that none of his own accomplishments, great as they might seem to others, have any lasting value.

• Finally, he says that the simplest things are really most important—enough to eat and drink and worthwhile work that satisfies the soul.

Vanity of the Cycle of Life and Death

3

Ecclesiastes 3

Before We Begin . . .

How do you feel about the well-known quotation "A time to be born, and a time to die"? Does this seem accurate to you, or is it too fatalistic?

Based on what you've read so far, do you think Solomon still seems to worship the true God? Or is he more of a skeptic or a fatalist?

Ecclesiastes 3

Everything Has Its Time

One of the most familiar passages from all of Ecclesiastes, if not the entire Bible, is chapter 3, verses 1–8. Let us look closely at the structure of this passage to see what is going on behind the words themselves.

First of all, note that verses 2–8 each contain two pairs of polar opposites, with each pair related to the other pair within the same verse. Or are they?

For example, in verse 2 Solomon contrasts birth and death, followed by planting and plucking. The first pair concerns the beginning and end of human life; the second pair deals with the same events in plant life.

But what about verse 5? How would you interpret "gathering" and "casting away" stones, in an era when people were sometimes executed by being stoned to death?

Read through these verses, as arranged by pairs in the following table. Then examine each pair and see if you can find any "linkage" between the two halves of each verse, as we have done for verse 2.

Verses/Pairs	Linkage
²A time to be born, and a time to die; A time to plant, and a time to pluck what is planted;	Birth and death of both animals and plants
³A time to kill, and a time to heal; A time to break down, and a time to build up;	
⁴A time to weep, and a time to laugh; A time to mourn, and a time to dance;	
⁵A time to cast away stones, and a time to gather stones; A time to embrace, and a time to refrain from embracing;	
⁶A time to gain, and a time to lose; A time to keep, and a time to throw away;	
⁷A time to tear, and a time to sew; A time to keep silence, and a time to speak;	
⁸A time to love, and a time to hate; A time of war, and a time of peace.	

Finally, note that Solomon has arranged this series of opposites in a multiple of seven, meaning seven groups of two. Seven is God's perfect number, usually suggesting completion.

Do you think Solomon thought he'd pretty much covered the territory? And, either way, what additional contrasts, perhaps more directly connected to modern life, might you suggest?

REALITY CHECK . . .

One important thing we mentioned earlier, in the introduction to this study guide, is that it simply is not possible to understand Ecclesiastes properly without reading and considering *all* of it before reaching any conclusions. This might be especially true of chapter 3, which can sound very pessimistic if you are not aware of Solomon's larger purpose. So, for those who cannot wait—meaning those who like to peek at the end of a book while they're still reading the beginning—chapter 11 ("Coming to a Close") includes a table that might help put a lot more of Ecclesiastes in perspective. If you go there now, pay special attention to the left column . . .

THE GOD-GIVEN TASK

Solomon began this chapter with a thesis—that everything has its proper time. He then illustrated it with the seven previous verses. Now he turns back to the question he started with, again asking, "What is the value of anyone's work?"

What three things does Solomon claim that God has done (v. 11)?

What does he then claim is man's appropriate response (v. 12)?

Finally, after explaining in verse 14 that God does what He does so that people should fear Him, how does Solomon conclude this section (v. 15)? What does he say that God will require of us?

INJUSTICE SEEMS TO PREVAIL

To wrap up this chapter of Ecclesiastes, in verses 16–22 Solomon does five main things:

1. He acknowledges that there is plenty of injustice in the world. Some scholars claim he did this to head off any objections to what he'd said just before, that God's creation is perfect and cannot be improved upon by man.

2. In verse 17 he acknowledges once again that God will "judge the righteous and the wicked, for there is a time there for every purpose and for every work."

3. He makes it clear one more time that men are like animals in a physical sense. Note that he is *not* talking about the soul, which sets man *apart* from the animals. Rather, he says that—just like animals—men come from the dust of the earth, breathe in the air, then eventually die and return to the dust. But again, he is *not* saying that men are no different from animals—only that they share many physical realities.

4. In verse 21 he asks a question that commentators have been trying to settle for centuries! Is he saying that man is directly connected to God (i.e., that man "goes upward" through his spirit), while animals simply return to the ground, or is he saying that man is truly different from animals, with a different destiny via man's spiritual connection with God? What do you think?

5. Finally, in verse 22 Solomon recommends that we enjoy life in what he appears to consider the *certain knowledge* that no one "can bring him [i.e., man] to see what will happen after him."

PULLING IT ALL TOGETHER . . .

• Chapter 3 of Ecclesiastes begins with what has been called one of the most eloquent passages of Scripture. It is a series of fourteen contrasts, structured in the "time for" mode.

• Next, Solomon points out that man should fear God, meaning that we should respect and worship Him.

• Finally, Solomon acknowledges rampant injustice here on earth, proclaims that God will judge everyone, and recommends that we enjoy life as best we can in spite of all the above.

Vanity of Life's Inequalities

4

Ecclesiastes 4

Before We Begin . . .

What do you think is the worst reason of all for driving yourself to be "successful" (meaning having lots of money and power) in the modern workplace? Whatever you feel this reason might be, do you think it was ever a factor in Solomon's world as well?

What about people who are "successful" without putting out much effort—for example, a modern celebrity who becomes "famous for being famous"? What advice would you want to give these people if you could get them all together?

Ecclesiastes 4

Chapter 4 begins with three verses that almost seem to go backwards. In contrast to the more positive sentiments at the end of chapter 3, Solomon seems to be rehashing some of the arguments he used earlier in favor of gloom and despair.

For example, what does Solomon say about the oppressed (v. 1)?

At the same time, who does he say has all the power?

Whom does he say he praised (v. 2)?

Finally, to bring this short section to a close, what does Solomon say about those who have never lived (v. 3)? Do you agree? Why do you think he would say such a thing at this point?

SOLOMON KNEW WHAT HE WAS TALKING ABOUT!

One of the "inappropriate motivators" Solomon identified in chapter 4 of Ecclesiastes is *envy*. Obviously, Solomon knew what he was talking about. We could easily search through the Bible and find numerous examples of the way that envy, all by itself, destroyed various people—or at least had a devastating effect on their lives. We could begin with the story of Cain, whose envy of Abel, his brother, led to murder. From there we might move forward to the stories of Jacob and Esau, of Joseph and his envious brothers, of Saul's self-destructive envy of David, and even of the Jewish leaders of Christ's own time, whose envy of His influence among "their" people led to His death on the Cross.

But what does the Bible itself say about envy? As you might expect, the book of Proverbs, also written by Solomon, mentions it several times but never in a positive light. The books of Job and Psalms mention it, too, as do the prophets Isaiah and Ezekiel.

But surprisingly, perhaps, the word *envy* occurs almost twice as many times in the New Testament as in the Old, even though the New is only about a third as long as the Old. Here are just a few examples, taken from Acts and from the epistles of Paul, James, and Peter.

But when the Jews saw the multitudes, they were filled with envy; and contradicting and blaspheming, they opposed the things spoken by Paul. (Acts 13:45 NKJV)

Let us walk properly, as in the day, not in revelry and drunkenness, not in lewdness and lust, not in strife and envy. (Rom. 13:13 NKJV)

You are still carnal. For where there are envy, strife, and divisions among you, are you not carnal and behaving like mere men? (1 Cor. 3:3 NKJV)

Love suffers long and is kind; love does not envy; love does not parade itself, is not puffed up. (1 Cor. 13:4 NKJV)

Let us not become conceited, provoking one another, envying one another. (Gal. 5:26 NKJV)

He is proud, knowing nothing, but is obsessed with disputes and arguments over words, from which come envy, strife, reviling, evil suspicions . . . (1 Tim. 6:4 NKJV)

We ourselves were also once foolish, disobedient, deceived, serving various lusts and pleasures, living in malice and envy, hateful and hating one another. (Titus 3:3 NKJV)

For where envy and self-seeking exist, confusion and every evil thing are there. (James 3:16 NKJV)

Therefore, laying aside all malice, all deceit, hypocrisy, envy, and all evil speaking . . . (1 Pet. 2:1 NKJV)

THE VANITY OF SELFISH TOIL

In verses 4–8 Solomon identifies two major "unfortunate" motivators that are as prevalent in the modern age as they were in his time. To help you identify these two bad reasons for doing things, we have arranged verses 4–8 into two groups in the following table. The challenge for you is to look around you, take stock of what you see in the modern workplace, then read Solomon's words carefully and identify the two faulty motivators he was talking about, which still drive people today. They sometimes move people into certain kinds of success but rarely move anyone into happiness. Take your time—this is a short exercise but not necessarily an easy one!

Solomon's Words	The Faulty Motivator
Again, I saw that for all toil and every skillful work a man is envied by his neighbor. This also is vanity and grasping for the wind. The fool folds his hands and consumes his own flesh. Better a handful with quietness than both hands full, together with toil and grasping for the wind. (Eccl. 4:4–6 NKJV)	
Then I returned, and I saw vanity under the sun: There is one alone, without companion: He has neither son nor brother. Yet there is no end to all his labors, nor is his eye satisfied with riches. But he never asks, "For whom do I toil and deprive myself of good?" This also is vanity and a grave misfortune. (Eccl. 4:7–8 NKJV)	

THE VALUE OF A FRIEND

In the next section, verses 9–12, Solomon offers what some consider one of the most hopeful insights of Ecclesiastes. What is his basic premise (v. 9)?

Have you ever heard this expression before? In what context? What is your earliest memory of hearing it? Have you said it yourself?

Solomon cites four advantages of making a friend and functioning as a team. List these advantages below.

1. _____

2. _____

3. _____

4. _____

Can you list ten additional advantages, off the top of your head, of working as a team in the modern world? What is the main advantage?

1. _____ 6. _____

2. _____ 7. _____

3. _____ 8. _____

4. _____ 9. _____

5. _____ 10. _____

Finally, in the second half of verse 12, Solomon says:

And a _____ cord is not quickly broken. (NKJV)

Fill in the blank in the verse above; in the space below, explain why you agree or disagree with Solomon on this point.

THE THREEFOLD CORD

Many a sermon has been preached—and several books have been written as well—on the threefold-cord concept that Solomon mentioned in Ecclesiastes 4:12: "And a threefold cord is not quickly broken."

Some sermons talk about diversity, unity, and cooperation; others talk about *body, spirit,* and *soul;* others break down *soul* into *mind, emotions,* and *will.* In each case, the message is that all the "parts" are needed to create the "whole" and give it a measure of strength greater than the sum of the parts.

Over the years, many thousands of ropes have been made of three separate strands woven together, because the three-strand design is always stronger than a single-strand rope of the same diameter. This assumes, of course, that you could get a single strand of the same thickness for comparison purposes, which would be impossible in many cases. Nonetheless, the principle still holds—if you want a strong polyester rope, don't make one gigantic strand of polyester; make three and twist them together! Or better yet, make hundreds of smaller ones, twist those together into three larger ones, then twist those together into one finished rope.

POPULARITY PASSES AWAY

The final section in this chapter, verses 13–16, has caused scholars more than a little bit of uncertainty over the years. And rereading the original language doesn't help much; when scholars go back to the original Hebrew, they can't be sure whether the pronoun "his" in verse 15 refers to the "poor and wise youth" or the "old and foolish king." Also, they can't be sure what the exact role of the "second youth" would be in verse 15. Even so, many scholars interpret this section in roughly the following way:

> *It's better to be "a poor and wise youth" who "comes out of prison to be king" than to be "an old and foolish king." Thus, the first youth in this story had many loyal subjects who loved him and approved of how he ruled their kingdom, even though he came from nowhere. However, he was eventually succeeded by someone else in whom the people would "not rejoice" (v. 16), perhaps meaning that they'd forgotten at least some of their own*

history. The last verse could also mean that the second youth was not a very accomplished ruler.

It's hard not to try to equate the youth who came "out of prison to be king" with Joseph, one of Solomon's celebrated ancestors, who rose from imprisonment under Pharaoh to a lofty position as second-in-command in the Egyptian kingdom. Yet in spite of Joseph's success, the pharaoh he served so well was eventually replaced and Joseph's critical role in saving Egypt from starvation was forgotten.

To make the comparison even more poignant, the children of Israel ("those who come afterward") eventually reviled even Moses, their greatest leader of all time, for leading them into temporary hardships on their way to the Promised Land.

In a larger sense, Solomon appears to be saying that any desire for power and popularity, like envy and greed, always leads to things that eventually become meaningless—what he calls "vanity and grasping for the wind."

PULLING IT ALL TOGETHER . . .

• Solomon begins this chapter by seeming to suggest that gloom and despair are reasonable responses to some of the situations he talked about in previous chapters.

• He then demonstrates that envy and greed always lead to negative results.

• Finally, he shows that grabbing for power and prestige also leads nowhere, meaning that all these things, *in themselves*, have no power whatsoever to edify, advance, or even briefly satisfy us. They all lead to failure of one kind or another.

VANITY OF RELIGION, POLITICS, AND RICHES

ECCLESIASTES 5:1–6:10

Before We Begin . . .

How do you feel about becoming rich—is it possible to accumulate great wealth yet still serve God above all else?

Do you feel that what we might call "earthly wisdom" will prevent us from making poor choices, especially in that to which we dedicate our lives? Is wisdom a help or a hindrance with respect to our relationships with God?

ECCLESIASTES 5

FEAR GOD, KEEP YOUR VOWS

Before we think about the first seven verses of chapter 5, let's take a look at the following passage from Deuteronomy:

> *When you make a vow to the LORD your God, you shall not delay to pay it; for the LORD your God will surely require it of you, and it would be sin to you. But if you abstain from vowing, it shall not be sin to you. That which has gone from your lips you shall keep and perform, for you voluntarily vowed to the LORD your God what you have promised with your mouth. (Deut. 23:21–23 NKJV)*

These words come from Moses' final speech to the children of Israel, delivered as they stood on the eastern shore of the Jordan River before they crossed over to occupy the land God had promised them. These words were part of an extended review of all the commandments and instructions the Lord had given the children of Israel earlier, combined with warnings and entreaties not to forget any of them.

It's important to remember the previous verses, and the earlier passages from the Bible that laid out the same things, because they help explain what Solomon was saying in Ecclesiastes 5:1–7. Contrary to what some commentators have suggested, these verses in Ecclesiastes probably were not intended as any kind of a "time-out" between the pieces of Solomon's overall argument against various futile pursuits (what he called "vanities"), which takes up much of Ecclesiastes.

For example, they probably were not intended only as advice on how to worship God, how to pray, and how to deal with vows, even though taking them that way is not completely wrong. But it's the big picture we're trying to focus on here, and in that larger sense Solomon was warning the original readers against things that were probably much more a part of their daily lives than they are of ours today.

Given the sacrificial system under which they were still worshiping, Solomon's original readers lived lives in which God would have been far more central than He is in many of our lives today. If they did even a small portion of what He commanded them, they would seldom be far away from something reminding them of His presence (see the sidebar "How Close Did God Stay to His Children?" in chapter 7 of this study guide).

Making rash vows, therefore, was right there at the top of the list of foolish mistakes they could make. Solomon called rash vows the "sacrifice of fools" in verse 1.

Just before he speaks of the "sacrifice of fools," what other advice does Solomon offer that would certainly be just as prudent today?

How would you phrase "draw near to hear rather than to give the sacrifice of fools" in modern language?

Based on the passage from Deuteronomy, quoted at the beginning of this study guide chapter, why do you think Solomon so clearly warned his readers not to be rash with their mouths?

LET THIS NOT BE A FOOLISH VOW!

One of the better-known vows that an ancient Israelite might take was called a *Nazirite* vow, from the Hebrew word *nazir,* meaning "consecrated." It could last for a month, a year, or even several years. In the case of Paul, who took a Nazirite vow as detailed in Acts 22:23–24 (and also referenced in Acts 18:18) to demonstrate to those who had begun to doubt that he was still a full-fledged Jew, it probably lasted a few months. In the case of someone such as Samson, who was dedicated as a Nazirite by his mother at his birth, it could last a lifetime.

To start a Nazirite vow, a person would shave all the hair off his or her head (yes, women could take the vow too). Some people would go so far as to shave every part of their bodies, including their arms and legs. Then they let all their hair grow back, without cutting any portion of it until the term of the vow was complete.

They also swore not to consume anything made from grapes, including juice, wine, and grape vinegar, or anything that included any derivative products of the grape in any amount whatsoever. Some also extended this prohibition to any intoxicating beverages at all, plus any vinegars made from apples or other sources. And if they failed to keep the terms at any point during the time period they'd agreed to, they were required to start over and do it all again from scratch.

The purpose of a Nazirite vow, as with the *tefillin* and *mezzuzot* mentioned elsewhere in this study guide, was to keep the person constantly aware of God. What could be more personal than literally thinking of God, and the vow you'd made to Him, every time you put something into your mouth?

What do you think Solomon means by the words "For God is in heaven, and you on earth" (v. 2)? What is he really talking about here?

Moving now to the summary of this section, what conclusion does Solomon draw that pulls this whole passage together yet also links directly to everything he has already written in Ecclesiastes (v. 7)?

THE VANITY OF GAIN AND HONOR

The meaning of verses 8–9 has been debated many times by many different scholars. The interpretation that seems most likely to reflect Solomon's intended meaning is that everyone in the official chain of command in Solomon's day, from the king himself on down to the lowest official, was engaged in plunder of one kind or another. And the object of all this plunder—as many people believe is also true of us today, via income and sales taxes—is what we might call the "common man."

Strangely enough, this might seem to be a self-incriminating statement. Solomon himself, as king, certainly brought a lot of money into his treasury by making financial demands on his subjects. But on the other hand, he might not have been referring to any specific royal hierarchy; more likely he was talking of "things in general."

Besides, who can doubt that a politician as wise as Solomon might be capable of saying one thing and doing another?

In verses 10–12, Solomon again returns to one of his main themes, that no matter how much a person has, he or she will never think it's enough! What does Solomon say that a lover of silver will never be satisfied with (v. 10)?

What does he say that a person who loves abundance will never be satisfied with?

In verse 11, what is the general principle Solomon is speaking of? How would you phrase it in more familiar English?

Likewise, how would you phrase verse 12 in more modern terms?

In verses 13–14, Solomon provides his own quick review of what he has just said. Read verse 13, reprinted below, and identify the conclusion he lays out in the second half (the words following the colon). Once again, how would you phrase this principle in more modern terms?

> *There is a severe evil which I have seen under the sun:*
> *Riches kept for their owner to his hurt.*
> *(Eccl. 5:13 NKJV)*

Verses 15–17, beginning with "As he came from his mother's womb, naked shall he return," lay out a principle that most of us have heard many times! What is a modern paraphrase of this verse?

Once again, after putting his finger on the eventual futility of working simply to build up a pile of possessions, Solomon shifts gears in the next several verses, which include most of chapter 6 of Ecclesiastes. As before, he recommends that we enjoy whatever God gives us—but he also includes several warnings along the way.

What does Solomon say is "good and fitting" for us to do (v. 18)?

What are the five things Solomon identifies as given by God (v. 19)?

1. _____

2. _____

3. _____

4. _____

5. _____

Why does Solomon say we should enjoy what God has given us (v. 20)—to keep us from doing what instead?

A True Story about a "Rash Vow"

Not so many years ago, in the mid-1970s, a young man from Detroit, Michigan, came to church and accepted Christ into his heart. The young man came from a poor family, had worked at simple jobs in the construction industry since he was a teen, and did not have much education because he'd been born with what we would now call a learning disability. In this fellow's case, even though he was not the least bit "stupid" in spite of what the other kids thought, he had a lot of trouble learning to read and never really mastered that critical skill.

In the months following his salvation, he became a devoted Christian, struggled to read his Bible as best he could, and learned to trust God totally. So when his church asked for annual pledges to fund a new missionary program, he wrote $3,000 on the pledge card, signed his name, and dropped it into the collection plate. The next day the minister called him into his office. With a big smile on his face, he said, "Brother, I think you might have made a mistake. You wrote down three thousand dollars, but I don't think you have that kind of money, do you? I suspect you left out the decimal, but don't worry—the Lord isn't going to hold you to it. So let's just change it to thirty dollars, shall we?"

The young man's jaw fell, and he jumped completely out of his chair. "Absolutely not! I wrote what I meant, and I'm going to trust God to provide it!"

In the year that followed, the young man received opportunity after opportunity to work extra hours and extra jobs. Three thousand dollars was a huge sum in those days, when top wages were still just a few dollars an hour, but the money kept coming in. And every month the young man made another payment of $250 on his pledge, which at that time was a bit more than his rent and his car payment combined.

At the end of that year, something remarkable happened to the young man. He wasn't very good at reading the instruction manuals and working the figures, but he'd learned how to work with all the tools and build houses from the ground up. During that same year he met a young woman who was also a Christian, fell in love, and got married just as the year came to an end. She worked in the same business, in the office of another construction company, so she had the kind of "book knowledge" of the industry that the young man himself had never mastered.

Within a few months after their marriage, they took a huge risk, inspired by the Lord. He quit his "safe" job and went into business for himself; his wife wrote up

A TRUE STORY ABOUT A "RASH VOW" (CONT.)

all his bids, he did the work, and she handled the billing, collecting, and other record keeping.

I think you know where this story is going, right? In the words of the young man himself, "The windows of heaven opened up and the blessings just poured out!" In a few years he wound up owning one of the largest and most successful construction companies in his whole area. He employed several other young men and women, many of whom couldn't get office jobs because they had his same handicap.

And, of course, he continued to give away most of his riches, as fast as they came in. In fact, they often came in faster than he could send them out, so eventually he had to employ people to help him give away the bounty God sent his way—simply for making a vow, trusting the Lord to help him keep it, and staying faithful through the "working out" of his walk of faith.

ECCLESIASTES 6:1–9

To continue what he started in 5:18, what warning does Solomon now include (v. 1)?

What is the inevitable result that Solomon identifies (v. 2)?

When we read verse 3, we must remember that children were considered wealth in Solomon's time. So what is Solomon saying in verses 3–6? Can you restate his point in modern English?

What does he mean by "All the labor of man is for his mouth" (v. 7)? How would you paraphrase this statement?

Finally, in verse 9 Solomon brings this short section to a close with the recommendation—once again—that we should be content with what we have. At the same time, the second half of verse 7, plus verses 8–9, simply reinforces Solomon's main point in this section by giving us additional insights. The whole three-verse passage might be restated as follows:

Verse 7: We work to keep ourselves alive, but earthly work does not satisfy our craving for a relationship with God.

Verse 8: Neither the wise nor the poor have any advantage over the foolish. A poor person might have street smarts and know how to get along, but he still has to deal with desires for material things that he can never satisfy.

Verse 9: It's better to settle for what is in front of you than to focus on empty dreams and keep longing for more.

Pulling It All Together . . .

• Solomon begins chapter 5 by warning the Israelites against failing to keep their vows to the Lord.

• Next, he virtually admits that most of the kings he knows—and their lower-level leaders as well—take more from the poor than they should.

• Solomon then finds several other ways to repeat some of what he has said earlier: (1) that no matter how much a person has, he or she will never think it's enough; (2) that the rich and the poor alike have no advantage over the foolish; and (3) that man always seems to concentrate on the physical and neglect the spiritual.

THE GOOD
AND THE BETTER

6

ECCLESIASTES 6:10–7:29

Before We Begin ...

Do you believe that Solomon teaches more by negative examples or by positive examples in the book of Ecclesiastes? What has been your experience so far? Do you think the previous pattern will continue?

What is your understanding of the expression "fear of the Lord"? What does it involve?

ECCLESIASTES 6:10–12

This three-verse fragment from chapter 6, coupled with chapter 7, introduces the second half of the book of Ecclesiastes. The major section of this half extends all the way through the middle of chapter 11, at which point we are almost to the end.

Here we find Solomon moving toward a far more positive conclusion. For several chapters he has been identifying the things that man "is not," or the things he "cannot know," or the inability of fame, wealth, good deeds, and other typical human pursuits to give meaning to our lives all by themselves. Now he begins to point toward things that we actually can do and things that we actually should seek. These are meaningful things that will make real differences in our spiritual lives, rather than cosmetic things that simply burnish our self-images or salve our consciences.

In other words, Solomon now begins to tell us how to worship and respect the one and only true God and how to live in ways that please Him.

Solomon conveys this advice in a series of statements often beginning with "It is good," or "A is better than B." At the same time, he also gives us a lot of clear-cut advice, in the form of suggestions, recommendations, and perhaps even a few commands.

Yet Solomon does not move instantly into a completely different mode. In chapters 7 and 8 especially we will find the expression "Who can find it out?" (Eccl. 7:24 NKJV) or an equivalent phrase, meaning that we will encounter many things we simply cannot understand *except by asking God.*

To set the scene, let us paraphrase the last three verses of chapter 6.

> *Whatever one is, he has been named already,*
> *For it is known that he is man;*
> *And he cannot contend with Him who is mightier*
> *than he. (v. 10 NKJV)*

Paraphrase: The world has already been created, and so have we. It's absolutely useless to try to argue with God about the way things should or shouldn't be. His decisions are absolute!

> *Since there are many things that increase vanity,*
> *How is man the better? (v. 11 NKJV)*

Paraphrase: It's very easy to pursue things that turn out to be foolish. So how can man recognize the will of God—the "better way" that God has provided?

> *For who knows what is good for man in life, all the days*
> *of his vain life which he passes like a shadow? Who can*
> *tell a man what will happen after him under the sun?*
> *(v. 12 NKJV)*

What Does It Mean to Fear the Lord?

Even as Solomon talked at length about acquiring true wisdom, he also referred to the "fear of the Lord" as though that were something we all should embrace. But why should we be afraid of God? Why would God, who is love, want us to fear Him?

The answer is painfully obvious. Fear of God does not mean trepidation. It does not mean that we should be afraid to encounter God in the same way we might be afraid to encounter a raging lion without a big-bore hunting rifle in our hands to balance the equation.

In the book of Proverbs, Solomon has a lot more to say about fearing the Lord. For example, in one famous passage, Solomon says:

> The fear of the LORD is the beginning of wisdom,
> And the knowledge of the Holy One is understanding.
> (Prov. 9:10 NKJV)

In other words, *fear of the Lord* and *wisdom* are linked very tightly together. But that's not all this well-known proverb says. In this verse, the word "fear" actually means "reverence." Those who fear God have reverence for Him; they stand in awe of Him. Yet if they have a positive relationship with God, they look forward to being in His presence.

Moses is an excellent example of one who feared God, yet he directly interacted with Him many, many times. All you have to do is read the book of Exodus to know that Moses depended on the wisdom of God, and he accomplished amazing things as a result.

But let us look once again at the proverb quoted above. The second half says, "And the knowledge of the Holy One is understanding." In other words, "fear of the LORD" in the first half of the verse means reverence for Him; it means honor and respect.

But reverence can be based only on *knowledge* of God. You can't honor and respect someone you know nothing about. But that same knowledge leads to *understanding,* and understanding then leads to *wisdom.*

To put all this another way, understanding tells us what is happening, while wisdom tells us why it is happening. Understanding gives us the facts, while wisdom tells us what to do with them. Understanding yields insight into how a problem might be solved, while wisdom tells us which solution to pursue and when and how to pursue it.

Paraphrase: On his own, man is utterly ignorant of God's plan for him—of his own unique place in the universe God has created.

And now that we have *that* settled, let's move on to the good news!

ECCLESIASTES 7

THE VALUE OF PRACTICAL WISDOM

In the following table, we have arranged the first fourteen verses of chapter 7, in their entirety, using the New King James Version of the Bible. The heading above says it all—these verses introduce a series of very practical bits of wisdom.

Your challenge is to read each verse, simplify it in your own words, and extract the gems of wisdom. Ask yourself, What is Solomon saying? What's the point? What plain meaning can we pull out of his often-poetic words? How might he say the same thing to us today if he were standing in front of us, teaching us what he has learned in modern English?

In many cases, Solomon might appear to be contradicting his own claim to wisdom, as in verse 3. How can it be better to cry than to laugh? The answer is probably contained in verse 14, which we have summarized for you in the second column of the table.

Note that our summary is quite a bit longer than the original verse, but this will *not* be the case for most of the others. At the same time, do not be fooled into thinking that this is a quick, easy exercise. It should be *very* rewarding, but it might take a bit of doing to reach a point at which you feel you've really *done* it. Note, also, that if you are using this guide in a group study, you might consider assigning different verses to different people (or to different groups of three or four people), then coming back together and sharing what you've learned.

Original Verse	In Your Own Words . . .
¹A good name is better than precious ointment, And the day of death than the day of one's birth;	
²Better to go to the house of mourning Than to go to the house of feasting, For that is the end of all men; And the living will take it to heart.	
³Sorrow is better than laughter, For by a sad countenance the heart is made better.	
⁴The heart of the wise is in the house of mourning, But the heart of fools is in the house of mirth.	
⁵It is better to hear the rebuke of the wise Than for a man to hear the song of fools.	
⁶For like the crackling of thorns under a pot, So is the laughter of the fool. This also is vanity.	
⁷Surely oppression destroys a wise man's reason, And a bribe debases the heart.	
⁸The end of a thing is better than its beginning; The patient in spirit is better than the proud in spirit.	
⁹Do not hasten in your spirit to be angry, For anger rests in the bosom of fools.	
¹⁰Do not say, "Why were the former days better than these?" For you do not inquire wisely concerning this.	
¹¹Wisdom is good with an inheritance, And profitable to those who see the sun.	
¹²For wisdom is a defense as money is a defense, But the excellence of knowledge is that wisdom gives life to those who have it.	
¹³Consider the work of God; For who can make straight what He has made crooked?	
¹⁴In the day of prosperity be joyful, But in the day of adversity consider: Surely God has appointed the one as well as the other, So that man can find out nothing that will come after him.	God creates both adversity and prosperity. Sometimes they are mixed together in ways that we cannot understand, especially if we try to predict our future by studying the present. Even so, we can often learn more from adversity than from prosperity. Above all else, we always need to *think* about whatever is happening and respond *wisely* to the events we cannot control.

What anomaly does Solomon point out (v. 15)?

What does he advise against in verse 16?

Do you think he means to imply that righteousness automatically destroys us? What would be a more reasonable interpretation?

What does he advise against in verse 17?

What does he say will happen to those who "fear God" (v. 18)?

In verse 20, Solomon mentions one of the foundational truths about salvation and forgiveness. What is that huge bit of truth/wisdom?

What does Solomon mean when he talks about hearing "your servant cursing you" (v. 21)? How does that fit together with verse 20? How can you tie it in with verse 21?

What limitation does Solomon acknowledge in verses 23–24? Would the same limitation apply to us in the modern age?

What task did Solomon assign himself (v. 25)?

In what sense do you think he means that "folly" is "wickedness" (v. 25)? Likewise with foolishness and madness—in what ways are these things "wicked"?

THE TRUE SOURCE OF WISDOM

One point that Solomon makes repeatedly throughout Ecclesiastes is that *human* wisdom isn't worth much in comparison to *godly* wisdom. The history of our world proves it over and over again. Human beings seldom see the whole picture, and even if they do, they seldom know exactly what to do about it. This is why Solomon points us toward God's wisdom over and over again.

What is the point, anyway, of trusting in a flawed system in which we try to comprehend everything on our own, when we can trust, instead, in the wisdom of the same all-knowing God who created everything that we often find so difficult and mysterious? In a sense, He also created all the possible *relationships* between all those things, and *understanding relationships* is what true wisdom is often all about.

Without tapping into God's wisdom, we simply cannot be wise in any real sense at all.

In verse 26, do you think Solomon is referring to an actual physical woman, or is he using "woman" to refer back to what he has just said in verse 25 about folly, foolishness, and madness?

Finally, what is the grand revelation that Solomon comes to at the end of this section (v. 29)?

Is this revelation positive or negative? Why?

What positive thing do you think "discovering" this truth might allow Solomon to do?

PULLING IT ALL TOGETHER . . .

• Here in the second half of Ecclesiastes, Solomon begins to give us much more positive input—more how-to advice rather than regrets over what doesn't work.

• Even so, Solomon continues to point out contradictions and anomalies.

• Solomon continually points toward one conclusion only—that fearing God and living accordingly is the only true path to happiness.

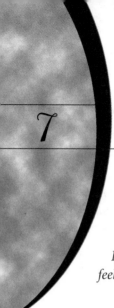

7

WISDOM

ECCLESIASTES 8

Before We Begin . . .

If you have heard of the "go along to get along" philosophy, how do you feel about it? To what extent should we do so in our modern culture?

Solomon often admits that he doesn't understand God's ways—how He works, why He allows certain things to happen, why certain people never seem to be punished. Does this mean Solomon is therefore a nonbeliever, or is he simply being honest about the questions that occur to him?

ECCLESIASTES 8

Ecclesiastes 8 is organized into two distinct halves. Verse 1 poses a question about a "wise man," followed by several more verses (2–9, equal to exactly half of the remaining 16) that show how a person might behave if he *were* that "wise man" of verse 1.

The second half of the chapter, verses 10–17, deals once again with the way that Solomon believes God intermixes punishment and reward—justice and *un*justice—in patterns that no one can comprehend via earthly wisdom. The result, of course, is that Solomon suggests the same course of action he endorsed in some of his earlier chapters.

Or does he? Let us look and see. Verse 1 begins by asking:

Who is like a wise man?

And who knows the interpretation of a thing?
A man's wisdom makes his face shine,
And the sternness of his face is changed.
(NKJV)

What do you think Solomon means in this verse? And what, if anything, does the second half of the verse, beginning with "A man's wisdom makes his face shine," have to do with the two questions in the first half?

Do you see any connection between the "face shine" comment above and what happened to Moses' face when he encountered God on Mount Sinai, as revealed in Exodus 34:29–30?

Perhaps even more important here, do you think Solomon is talking about a man who is extremely wise in all things (such as himself), or do you think is he talking more about common sense—perhaps what we might call "street smarts" in today's terms?

OBEY AUTHORITIES FOR GOD'S SAKE

In verse 2, Solomon makes plain his own position on obeying earthly authorities. Interestingly enough, verse 2 sounds very similar to three separate recountings of an event in the life of Christ, as recorded in Matthew 22:21, Mark 12:17, and Luke 20:25. In the Matthew account, the corresponding section reads like this:

"Render therefore to Caesar the things that are Caesar's, and to God the things that are God's." (Matt. 22:21 NKJV)

The similar verse from Ecclesiastes reads like this:

I say, "Keep the king's commandment for the sake of your oath to God." (Eccl. 8:2 NKJV)

What is your opinion with respect to these two verses? Are they saying essentially the same thing, or did Solomon have in mind something quite different from what Jesus was saying?

In verse 3, what is meant by "Do not be hasty to go from his presence"? (Bear in mind that this verse is talking about a worldly king, not God.) How could being too hasty be a problem for someone of Solomon's time?

Also consider the statement "Do not take your stand for an evil thing." Could adopting an unpopular cause, especially one the king did not favor, be considered rebellious—or worse?

What is the overall lesson taught by these three verses? That is, a wise man knows what? Or knows how to do what?

The next two groups of verses teach additional principles about how to "get along" in life here on earth; these principles are just as apropos today as they were in Solomon's time. Read the following verse and write on the blank below it the basic principle that it teaches. Do the same with verses 5–7.

> *Where the word of a king is, there is power;*
> *And who may say to him, "What are you doing?"*
> *(Eccl. 8:4 NKJV)*

Basic Principle: _____

> *He who keeps his command will experience nothing harmful;*
> *And a wise man's heart discerns both time and judgment,*
> *Because for every matter there is a time and judgment,*
> *Though the misery of man increases greatly.*
> *For he does not know what will happen;*
> *So who can tell him when it will occur?*
> *(Eccl. 8:5–7 NKJV)*

Basic Principle: _____

Verse 8 reinforces what has gone before by reminding us that we do not have the power to delay our own deaths ("No one has power over the spirit to retain the spirit"), modern medical science notwithstanding. Likewise, no one has any way to be released from "that war" or any way to escape the inevitable result of his own wickedness.

Finally, Solomon summarizes this brief section in verse 9, in a roundabout way, by saying, "There is a time in which one man rules over another to his own hurt."

But such a thing will not happen to those who observe the basic principle outlined in verses 5–7. This principle might be restated as "Do what is honorable and acceptable within your community, for this is a good way to stay out of trouble."

HOW CLOSE DID GOD STAY TO HIS CHILDREN?

Earlier in this study guide we said that the children of Israel would seldom be far away from something reminding them of God's presence if they did as He commanded them. This brings up an obvious question: What were the ancient Jews commanded to do—which modern Christians generally do *not* do—to keep His presence ever before them?

One of the best-known of all the ancient Jewish prayers is called the *Shema* (or *Sh'ma*), which begins with Deuteronomy 6:4. Verses 5–9, which are often called the *V'ahavta* portion because verse 7 starts with that word, are also part of most recitations of the Shema, so that the two sections are really more like one. Various groups (i.e., Reform, Conservative, etc.) within Judaism may or may not add two additional sections, one from the eleventh chapter of Deuteronomy and another from the book of Numbers.

Here is the basic text, which everyone seems to agree is part of the Shema:

"Hear, O Israel: The LORD our God, the LORD is one!

[Here, most Jews insert a variation of the words "Bless His name and His glorious kingdom, forever and ever." This portion originated in the ancient temple services. Nowadays, to indicate that it does not come directly from Scripture, it is usually recited very quietly. The biblical text then continues . . .]

"You shall love the LORD your God with all your heart, with all your soul, and with all your strength.

"And these words which I command you today shall be in your heart. You shall teach them diligently to your children, and shall talk of them when you sit in your house, when you walk by the way, when you lie down, and when you rise up. You shall bind them as a sign on your hand, and they shall be as frontlets between your eyes. You shall write them on the doorposts of your house and on your gates. (Deut. 6:4–9 NKJV)

In addition to reciting the Shema at least twice daily, many devout Jews still wear *tefillin* (pronounced *teh-feel'-in*) when they pray, to honor the command in verse 8. They also put *mezzuzot* (pronounced *meh'-zoo-zoat*; mezzuzah in the singular) on their doorjambs to honor the command in verse 9.

(Note that *tefillin* are small leather boxes containing short passages of Scripture; they are fastened on the arm and on the head with long leather thongs. *Mezzuzot* are small elongated boxes, made of metal, ceramic, and other materials, that contain tiny portions of Scripture; they are situated on doorjambs, where they can be touched by anyone entering or leaving the house.)

DEATH COMES TO ALL

What does verse 10 tell us about what happens to the wicked? Do you think Solomon is still talking about judgment as delivered by an earthly ruler, or is this a reference to divine judgment?

What anomaly does Solomon point out in verse 11? What is the result?

What is the contrast between those who do evil and those who "fear God" (v. 12)?

In verse 13, Solomon seems to be contradicting himself (especially what he wrote in verse 11) when he says that the wicked will not "prolong his days." But he is talking about what "days"? Does he mean mortal or immortal life? Life on earth or life in heaven?

What does Solomon say yet again, in verse 14, about divine retribution? (Hint: If you translate the word "vanity" as "meaningless," you'll get a slightly different take.)

In the last three verses of this chapter (vv. 15–17), Solomon returns once again to familiar territory. For example, here is what verse 15 says:

So I commended enjoyment, because a man has nothing better under the sun than to eat, drink, and be merry; for this will remain with him in his labor all the days of his life which God gives him under the sun. (NKJV)

How would you paraphrase this familiar verse? More important, what do you think Solomon's deeper meaning is here? Use the space below to answer these two questions. Then, if you are not familiar with the word "hedonism," look it up and decide whether Solomon really embraced that philosophy. Then answer the "Hedonism—Yes or No?" question below.

Hedonism—Yes or No? _____

How do you think most people interpret verse 15? Do they see a deeper meaning, or do they read it as permission to do as they wish and not worry about the consequences?

Finally, read verses 16–17 very carefully:

When I applied my heart to know wisdom and to see the business that is done on earth, even though one sees no sleep day or night, then I saw all the work of God, that a man cannot find out the work that is done under the sun. For though a man labors to discover it, yet he will not find it; moreover, though a wise man attempts to know it, he will not be able to find it. (NKJV)

How would you summarize these two verses? Again, what is Solomon really saying here? Is he "giving up" on God, or is he saying something else entirely?

PULLING IT ALL TOGETHER . . .

• Solomon begins this chapter by talking about a wise man— but not necessarily a sage.

• He then makes it clear that he is talking about someone with "street smarts," someone who knows how to get along with earthly authorities.

• Solomon's point about *going along to get along,* to put it in more modern terms, is somewhat similar to what Christ said about *rendering unto Caesar the things that are Caesar's,* although Solomon and Christ came at the same "general truth" from different perspectives.

• Solomon ends the chapter by suggesting that we should enjoy our lives here on earth as much as possible but that we should keep ourselves in tune with God and His will for our lives. For no one can understand God's ways from an earthly perspective, but God still rules every aspect of His magnificent creation—including us!

8   ENJOYING LIFE

ECCLESIASTES 9:1–10:1

Before We Begin...

What is your impression of the value Solomon places on wisdom up to this point?

What about his views on enjoying life—first, based on what you've read so far, what do you think he would say about the subject? And second, would you agree with him?

ECCLESIASTES 9

With chapter 9, Solomon begins a section of Ecclesiastes that extends through the midpoint of chapter 11. If we had to label this section, we might suggest that its main theme seems to be "None of us really know what will happen to us." In the very first verse, Solomon states this quite clearly:

> *For I considered all this in my heart, so that I could declare it all: that the righteous and the wise and their works are in the hand of God. People know neither love nor hatred by anything they see before them. (NKJV)*

In other words, none of us are truly in charge of our own lives. We can't predict what is coming by looking around us; indeed, it is much easier to predict the weather than our own future!

At the same time, our ignorance of God's plans and purposes does not make Him any less sovereign. It simply means that we will not always understand what is happening to us and to others around us.

The flip side of that equation, of course, is that those who walk closely with God, and truly trust Him with all the details of their lives, almost always live lives of enormous meaning, excitement, and fulfillment. What better purpose could our lives have than to be used by God in bringing about His divine plan, no matter how tiny and seemingly insignificant our "moment on stage" might be? The key lies in surrendering to God's will, which remains one of the most difficult things for many of us to do.

Verse 2 begins with a phrase that many commentators believe relates directly back to verse 1. In that interpretation, the statement "All things come alike to all" simply amplifies verse 1. But we really don't have to choose an interpretation, for the same statement can look both ways. In other words, even though we don't know our own fate, we know that we all will be subject to the same kinds of things. This truth points to the "one event" mentioned in verse 2.

What are the seven categories of people to whom Solomon says "one event happens" (v. 2)? We have included verse 2 below for reference. Write the seven categories in the numbered blanks provided below.

> *One event happens to the righteous and the wicked;*
> *To the good, the clean, and the unclean;*
> *To him who sacrifices and him who does not sacrifice.*
> *As is the good, so is the sinner;*
> *He who takes an oath as he who fears an oath.*
> *(NKJV)*

1. _____   5. _____

2. _____   6. _____

3. _____   7. _____

4. _____

(Hint: The statement that Solomon adds near the end of verse 2, "As is the good, so is the sinner," should not be included in your list of categories. This is essentially a summary of everything he is saying in this passage, meaning that "the rain falls on the just and the unjust," to paraphrase another famous quotation!)

The Difference between Faith and Trust

The words *faith* and *trust* are completely absent from the book of Ecclesiastes, at least in the New King James Version. Yet that does not mean the *concepts* are missing as well. On the contrary, Solomon often seems to be aware of the fundamental difference between the two words, even as he also makes it plain that both faith and trust in God are essential to all who walk "under the sun."

What is that "fundamental difference," anyway? Aren't faith and trust really the same thing?

It might be easier to see the difference if we look at the words themselves as parts of speech. Faith is a noun, and by definition a noun is the name of a person, place, or thing. In this case, faith is a "thing," but it is also an *abstract* thing. You can't put a box of faith on the table; you can't hand faith to someone else or put three pounds of it in a package and ship it to Philadelphia. As the writer of Hebrews said, "Now faith is the substance of things hoped for, the evidence of things not seen" (Heb. 11:1 NKJV). This doesn't sound like anything you could hold in your hand.

In contrast, although trust can also be a noun, in the faith/trust dynamic we have to think of it only as a verb. And a verb, by definition, is a word that denotes action.

In other words, you can "trust" God, but you can't "faith" God. And that requirement to do something on your own, to move from having faith to putting your trust in God, makes all the difference in the world.

This is especially true when you do things as a direct result of your trust. For example, you don't quit your regular job, sell your belongings, and move to the Sudan to minister to the natives "on faith"; you do it because you've gone beyond simple faith and are now trusting in God to achieve His purposes through your actions.

Faith is passive; it's hopeful; it involves waiting on the Lord. Trust is active; it's bold and sure; it involves *doing* what He tells you, not *waiting* to be told what the outcome will be.

In verse 3 Solomon again summarizes everything he has just said. Here are some of the lessons he seems to be putting in front of us in this verse, paraphrased (with additional explanations) line by line in the second column of the table below.

Ecclesiastes 9:3 NKJV	Modern Paraphrase
This is an evil in all that is done under the sun: that one thing happens to all.	The sad part of all the above (i.e., the "evil in all that is done under the sun") is that since we all seem to share the same fate (or so it seems, based on our limited vision of eternal reality) . . .
Truly the hearts of the sons of men are full of evil; madness is in their hearts while they live,	most people react to their inability to control things and to determine their own destiny, via worldly means, by embracing "evil" (i.e., sin) in all its forms, which often looks like a form of madness yet . . .
and after that they go to the dead.	still leads to the same fate, whether we live sin-filled or sin-free lives: that is, we all eventually die.

So far, things are not looking too good, according to Solomon! However, he immediately says that even though we are all subject to the same fortunes and failures of life on earth, while we are still alive we should not despair—"for a living dog is better than a dead lion" (Eccl. 9:4 NKJV).

Given that in Solomon's era, dogs were generally despised and lions were generally honored, what is the deeper meaning of verse 4?

What does Solomon say is known by the living (v. 5)?

What does he say is known by the dead?

What do the dead have, and why?

What three things does Solomon say "have now perished" (v. 6)?

What does he say they will therefore "nevermore" have a share in?

To what does the phrase "under the sun" actually refer?

What two things does Solomon suggest we should do (v. 7)? Why does he say we should do these things?

In verses 8–9 Solomon tells us to enjoy life as God enables us to do so. In verse 10 he encourages us to work diligently at whatever we are able to do.

What color does Solomon suggest that our garments should be (v. 8)?

What does he mean by "Let your head lack no oil"? To what ancient desert custom does this verse refer?

What does Solomon recommend in terms of the person with whom we live (v. 9)?

Why does Solomon say that we should do whatever our hand finds to do (v. 10), which essentially means to pursue any labor God enables us to pursue?

The following passage is so familiar that you might very well be able to fill in the blanks, in the version below, without looking in your Bible! But even if you can, check yourself to make sure every word is correct according to the New King James Version.

I returned and saw under the _____ that—
The race is not to the _____,
Nor the _____ to the strong,

DID SOLOMON INCLUDE CONTRADICTIONS IN ECCLESIASTES?

The question, did Solomon include contradictions in Ecclesiastes? can probably never be answered to everyone's satisfaction. Nearly three thousand years later, some still see contradictions where others see harmony. A good case in point might be Ecclesiastes 4:2–3 versus Ecclesiastes 9:4–6. Here are the two passages, side by side.

Ecclesiastes 4:2–3 NKJV	Ecclesiastes 9:4–6 NKJV
Therefore I praised the dead who were already dead, more than the living who are still alive. Yet, better than both is he who has never existed, who has not seen the evil work that is done under the sun.	But for him who is joined to all the living there is hope, for a living dog is better than a dead lion. For the living know that they will die; but the dead know nothing, and they have no more reward, for the memory of them is forgotten. Also their love, their hatred, and their envy have now perished; nevermore will they have a share in anything done under the sun.

Is Solomon saying that the dead are better off than the living, as in the earlier example, or is he saying that it's always better to remain alive, as in the later example? The most likely answer is that he is looking at life and death from two different perspectives.

In the passage from chapter 4, Solomon is probably saying that someone under intense pressure, who has seen the overwhelming evil that exists "under the sun" and wishes he could avoid it, might feel that he would be better off dead. Certainly this sentiment is a major reason for the high rates of suicide in many modern societies.

On the other hand, in the passage from chapter 9, Solomon is saying that, once dead, a person has no chance to enjoy life in any way whatsoever. But life in even the most oppressive conditions, in general, is better than death—if for no other reason than the possibility that things will eventually turn around.

This latter thought is one that Solomon repeats and reemphasizes in many different ways throughout Ecclesiastes, especially as he nears the end of the book. We cannot control all the random forces that surround us, but logically speaking, we're probably just as likely to see things get better as we are to see them get worse.

Nor bread to the _____,
Nor _____ to men of understanding,
Nor favor to men of _____;
But _____ and _____ happen to them all.
For man also does not know his _____:
Like fish taken in a cruel _____,
Like _____ caught in a snare,
So the sons of men are snared in an evil time,
When it falls suddenly upon them.
(Eccl. 9:11–12 NKJV)

WISDOM SUPERIOR TO FOLLY

In verses 13–15 Solomon tells a story that he obviously considered a prime example of ingratitude, further reinforcing his argument that wisdom, in and of itself, has almost no value. As you read these verses, be aware that the word "remembered," in verse 15, carries with it the meaning of "rewarded." In fact, the Bible lists a number of "God remembered" moments, involving Noah, Abraham, Rachel, and Hannah, to name just a few. In many cases, "remembering" involved keeping a promise (as when God remembered his covenant) or providing a reward.

Whom do you think Solomon might be talking about? Do you know of any similar situations in ancient history (not necessarily from Solomon's time) that he might have been referring to?

Look up the following passages and fill in the blanks below to discover Solomon's conclusion.

Then I said:
"Wisdom is better than _____.
Nevertheless the poor man's wisdom is _____,
And his _____ are not heard.

Words of the wise, spoken quietly, should be heard
Rather than the _____ of a ruler of fools.
Wisdom is better than _____ of war;
But one sinner _____ much good."
(Eccl. 9:16–18 NKJV)

Dead flies putrefy the perfumer's _____,
And cause it to give off a foul _____;
So does a little folly to one respected for wisdom and
_____. (Eccl. 10:1 NKJV)

ECCLESIASTES 10:1

As the above passages show, the first verse of chapter 10 belongs with the last verse of chapter 9, because it concludes the original thought in an especially graphic way. Apparently, it wasn't as easy to keep dead flies from accumulating in a bottle of ointment in Solomon's time as it might be today!

PULLING IT ALL TOGETHER . . .

• Solomon begins this chapter by observing—once again— that none of us know much about the future.

• He then makes it clear that it is still better to be alive than dead, no matter how difficult things can get.

• Solomon advises us to enjoy life as much as we can, within our abilities and our situations, as given to us by God.

• Ultimately, Solomon says that wisdom is still better than foolishness even though it doesn't necessarily pay better, either in material goods or in recognition and approval.

THE WISE AND THE FOOLISH

9

ECCLESIASTES 10:2–11:6

Before We Begin . . .

Who is the wisest person you have ever known? Why?

Without naming names, who is the most foolish person you have ever known? Why?

ECCLESIASTES 10:2–20

In the first section of chapter 10, verses 2–7, Solomon gives a series of examples that illustrates what can happen, even to a wise man, if his "ruler" pursues various follies of his own. In other words, being wise and acting accordingly aren't always enough!

In verse 2 Solomon says, "A wise man's heart is at his right hand, but a fool's heart at his left." Remembering that in the Bible the right hand is often considered the hand of strength and honor, what do you think this comparison (which comes from a Hebrew idiom and has absolutely nothing to do with modern political parties!) actually means?

How would someone demonstrate that he is a fool, even as he simply "walks along the way" (v. 3)? Do foolish people walk differently?

What does Solomon say resolves many crises by "pacifying great offenses" (v. 4)?

To further expand on the above, what does conciliation have to do with leaving (or not leaving) your post? How would you restate this verse in modern English?

How does the quotation below, also by Solomon but from another book in the Bible, fit in with the above discussion?

> *As messengers of death is the king's wrath,*
> *But a wise man will appease it.*
> *(Prov. 16:14 NKJV)*

Verses 5–7 all relate to the same scenario, which Solomon turns into a personal statement by claiming that he has seen it happen himself. In the table below, we have arranged the three verses in the left column, with space in the column on the right for a modern paraphrase. We have paraphrased the first verse; your challenge is to do the same with the two that remain.

Ecclesiastes 10:5–7 NKJV	Modern Paraphrase
There is an evil I have seen under the sun, As an error proceeding from the ruler:	I have seen men in positions of power make serious mistakes.
Folly is set in great dignity, While the rich sit in a lowly place.	
I have seen servants on horses, While princes walk on the ground like servants.	

Verses 8–11 all relate to similar scenarios. The first two verses involve events that most likely would be completely accidental. For example, in verse 8, what can happen accidentally to someone who digs a hole?

What about someone who breaks through a wall, or a fence? What can happen to him?

Likewise, in the first half of verse 9, what can happen to someone who is "quarrying stones"—that is, chopping them out of the ground for use as building blocks, or perhaps just moving them out of the way to plant a field?

The last half of verse 9 ties in with verse 10. First, what does verse 9 tell us can happen to anyone who splits wood?

On the other hand, what would a wise man do, according to verse 10, to avoid the problem implied in verse 9—or at least to minimize the possibility?

In verse 11, the last verse of this section, Solomon presents an interesting contrast. The message appears to be that timing is everything, for a snake might bite before it is charmed but be perfectly safe after it has been charmed. And a babbler, of course, knows nothing of the value of good timing; he is just as likely to speak out of turn as he would be to speak at the proper moment.

BUT WE STILL DON'T KNOW THE FUTURE!

The last nine verses of chapter 10 break down into two main sections, each one emphasizing how risky it can be to (1) speak foolishly and (2) criticize others, especially people in charge.

To see what Solomon has to say about speaking foolishly, fill in the blanks in verses 12–15 below.

> *The words of a wise man's mouth are _____,*
> *But the lips of a fool shall _____ him up;*
> *The words of his mouth begin with _____,*
> *And the end of his _____ is raving madness.*
> *A fool also multiplies _____.*
> *No man knows what is to be;*
> *Who can tell him what will be after him?*
> *The labor of fools _____ them,*
> *For they do not even know how to go to the city!*
> *(NKJV)*

CAST YOUR BREAD UPON THE WATERS

The generally accepted meaning of this familiar expression, from Ecclesiastes 11:1, is that we should always try to do good deeds for others with no thought of repayment or "increase" of any kind. But we should not be surprised if repayment comes along at some point, often many years later.

Two simple examples. A minister once spoke about counseling a young lady and helping her through some severe spiritual difficulties. Her last name was a bit unusual—yet it rang a bell in his memory. For a day or two he couldn't figure out why, but then it suddenly hit him. He'd been in the hospital thirty years earlier and had shared a room with a man with the same last name. That man's father came to visit one day and wound up sharing the gospel with the younger man, who then accepted Christ and eventually went into the ministry himself.

You guessed it—the young lady turned out to be the daughter of the young man with whom the minister had shared that hospital room so many years earlier—and the granddaughter of the man who led him to Christ.

Another young minister talked of inviting a college student home for dinner after services one Sunday. The student was a young man the minister had never met before, but he looked hungry and lonely and did not look like he could afford to buy many good lunches for himself.

Again, an unusual name, and again, a total blank until a day or two later. Then it hit the minister. Once when he was in seminary, his cash supply had dwindled to $11, with nothing on the horizon, in the way of eating money, for several weeks. On that very day he was invited for lunch, and then dinner, by one of the families in the church he attended. They lived close to his dorm, and they wound up inviting him over many times after that.

Once more you guessed it. The young college student was the son of the man who'd invited the minister for lunch so many years earlier, before the son was even born. And in the same fashion, the minister wound up inviting the young man into his home, his family, and eventually his heart as well.

"Cast your bread upon the waters, *for you will find it after many days.*"

Verses 16–19 are like proverbs, which is not too surprising since Solomon wrote the book of Proverbs as well. In verse 16, is he saying that the king is a child in a chronological sense, or does he mean something else? In what other sense could a king be a child?

What does he say would be a proper reason for feasting (v. 17)?

Why would having a king who was "the son of nobles" make any kind of a difference?

Why does Solomon say that a building can decay, or a house can leak (v. 18)?

What is a feast made for (v. 19)? And what helps bring laughter into the picture?

This section ends with a warning not to curse either a ruler or the rich, even in our thoughts and even in the privacy of our own bedrooms. Why does Solomon say that this would be a bad idea?

Do you agree with the gist of what he is saying here, even if you don't accept the bird metaphors?

DID HE SAY "BREAD" OR "SEED"?

Is it possible that the expression "Cast your bread upon the waters" had a literal meaning in Solomon's day? Perhaps not, but on the other hand, "Cast your *seed* upon the water" undoubtedly did.

In those days the Jordan River often overflowed its banks, flooding all the nearby fields. When that happened, if the seasonal timing was right, farmers who knew the ways of the river would often climb into small boats and row or pole their way over their fields. And then, while the boat was still moving (perhaps even rowed by someone else, if the boat were big enough), they would sow their seed by casting it on the water, just as they would do if they had been walking across a dry field.

Why? Well, as the waters receded, they would deposit a layer of nutrient-rich silt right over the top of the heavier seed, which would fall to the bottom and be covered up. The result would be a perfectly fertilized crop that often would be far more bountiful than one planted in the more typical "dry" fashion.

ECCLESIASTES 11:1–6

THE VALUE OF DILIGENCE

In the sidebar regarding the first verse of chapter 11 ("Cast Your Bread upon the Waters," elsewhere in this chapter), we indicated that the "generally accepted meaning of this familiar expression" is positive. We should do good things even though we know that many will not be rewarded.

But this interpretation could be a little different from what Solomon had in mind. A more accurate treatment from his standpoint might be that we should simply *do* the normal things that are part of our daily lives. Sow your seed, he says, whether the wind is blowing or not! Reap your crops, he says, whether the skies are clear or full of clouds!

In other words, don't let everything you do depend on what's going on around you. That doesn't mean you should always ignore the weather, your physical condition, or a thousand other things—but in general, stop sniffing the wind, pawing the ground, or waiting for Christmas! Get on with it! Plant your fields! Bring in your crops!

Behave as though tomorrow was coming for sure.

Or, as the Lord advised the children of Israel through the prophet Jeremiah, many years later, when they were just beginning their 490 years of captivity in Babylon:

> *Build houses and dwell in them; plant gardens and eat their fruit. Take wives and beget sons and daughters; and take wives for your sons and give your daughters to husbands, so that they may bear sons and daughters— that you may be increased there, and not diminished. And seek the peace of the city where I have caused you to be carried away captive, and pray to the LORD for it; for in its peace you will have peace. (Jer. 29:5–7 NKJV)*

In Solomon's view, we have no control over the future and no way of knowing how anything we do will turn out, no matter how carefully we try to do damage control in advance.

Here are Solomon's first and last words on the subject, taken from this particular six-verse passage. If you had to extract Solomon's main message in fifty words or less, you could not do better than simply linking verse 1 and verse 6 directly together.

> *Cast your bread upon the waters,*
> *For you will find it after many days. . . .*
> *In the morning sow your seed,*

And in the evening do not withhold your hand;
For you do not know which will prosper,
Either this or that,
Or whether both alike will be good.
(Eccl. 11:1, 6 NKJV)

PULLING IT ALL TOGETHER . . .

- Solomon begins this section by suggesting that not all people in positions of power act wisely all the time.

- He then advises us to make sure we live up to our own obligations by acting responsibly, even when others do not.

- Next, Solomon lists some of the things that can happen to us even when we try our hardest to be mature, dependable, and accountable.

- Finally, he points out once again that we have no way of knowing the future, and therefore we would do well to be cautious and diligent at all times.

10

SPREADING THE GOOD AND THE BEST

ECCLESIASTES 11:7–12:14

Before We Begin . . .

If you had to condense Solomon's main message in your own words before reading any further—perhaps in just one sentence—could you do it? What does he say that we should do above all else? (Note: If this exercise seems too uncertain at this point, come back to this question when you've finished this chapter.)

If you are planning to enjoy life, when do you think you should start?

ECCLESIASTES 11:7–12:7

The next major portion of Ecclesiastes, beginning with 11:7 and extending through 12:7, contains three main parts. In no particular order, those parts include

- a call to make sure we enjoy life while we are young, because old age brings a gradual decline in our bodies, our minds, and our attitudes;

- a call to enjoy life as much as we can, for death is coming for us all; and

- a call to begin early to enjoy life, because youth doesn't last long. However, we should still live conscientiously and sensibly, with as much maturity as possible.

Your first challenge is to read each of the following passages from Ecclesiastes, reprinted but separated into the three sections corresponding to the above bullet points. Consider the main message of each passage in its entirety, then assign one of the bullet points to it by writing the first five words of the bullet point on the blank below the biblical passage, after the words "This sections corresponds to . . ." Then respond to the questions that follow.

> *Truly the light is sweet,*
> *And it is pleasant for the eyes to behold the sun;*
> *But if a man lives many years*
> *And rejoices in them all,*
> *Yet let him remember the days of darkness,*
> *For they will be many.*
> *All that is coming is vanity.*
> *(Eccl. 11:7–8 NKJV)*

This section corresponds to _____

> *Rejoice, O young man, in your youth,*
> *And let your heart cheer you in the days of your youth;*
> *Walk in the ways of your heart,*
> *And in the sight of your eyes;*
> *But know that for all these*
> *God will bring you into judgment.*
> *Therefore remove sorrow from your heart,*
> *And put away evil from your flesh,*
> *For childhood and youth are vanity.*
> *(Eccl. 11:9–10 NKJV)*

This section corresponds to _____

> *Remember now your Creator in the days of your*
> *youth,*
> *Before the difficult days come,*
> *And the years draw near when you say,*
> *"I have no pleasure in them":*
> *While the sun and the light,*
> *The moon and the stars,*
> *Are not darkened,*

And the clouds do not return after the rain;
In the day when the keepers of the house tremble,
And the strong men bow down;
When the grinders cease because they are few,
And those that look through the windows grow dim;
When the doors are shut in the streets,
And the sound of grinding is low;
When one rises up at the sound of a bird,
And all the daughters of music are brought low.
Also they are afraid of height,
And of terrors in the way;
When the almond tree blossoms,
The grasshopper is a burden,
And desire fails.
For man goes to his eternal home,
And the mourners go about the streets.

Remember your Creator before the silver cord is loosed,
Or the golden bowl is broken,
Or the pitcher shattered at the fountain,
Or the wheel broken at the well.
Then the dust will return to the earth as it was,
And the spirit will return to God who gave it.
(Eccl. 12:1–7 NKJV)

This section corresponds to _____

From any of the three sections you have read and ranked above, what would you consider the most memorable passage? This need not necessarily be the most familiar passage—rather, which one did you personally like the most?

What does Solomon mean by "days of darkness" in 11:8?

What does he mean by "grinders" in 12:3?

What does he mean by "before the silver cord is loosed" in 12:6?

Finally, what imagery is he invoking in 12:6, when he talks about a gold bowl, a pitcher, and a wheel?

THE WHOLE DUTY OF MAN

The words "Whole Duty of Man" do not appear in the text of the New King James Version (NKJV), which we have used as the source for the Scripture quotations in this study guide. However, the words do appear in a heading in the NKJV, inserted by the translators just before verse 8 in chapter 12.

On the other hand, those exact words do appear in the text of Ecclesiastes 12:13 in the New International Version (NIV) and the King James Version (KJV). Because of its age (almost four hundred years), the KJV is most likely the source for the frequent appearance of those words in so many places today.

Any number of students, philosophers, and social engineers have put forth their own versions of "the whole duty of man" over the centuries. Without reading all their efforts, it is impossible to say who comes the closest to the truth, but we don't have that problem with what Solomon said. Certainly, from God's perspective, it is our "whole duty" to treat Him with respect and obey His commandments.

Anything less would be the *infinite foolishness* of which Solomon spoke so often, and so eloquently, in the book of Ecclesiastes.

THE WHOLE DUTY OF MAN

In the last seven verses of the book of Ecclesiastes, Solomon repeats one of his main themes. He also recommends, once again, two things he mentioned earlier.

Please read these concluding verses below. Then, using the blanks provided, identify the theme and the two recommendations. Finally, answer the questions about the identity and the qualifications of the author himself.

> *"Vanity of vanities," says the Preacher,*
> *"All is vanity."*
>
> *And moreover, because the Preacher was wise, he still taught the people knowledge; yes, he pondered and sought out and set in order many proverbs. The Preacher sought to find acceptable words; and what was written was upright—words of truth.*
>
> *The words of the wise are like goads, and the words of scholars are like well-driven nails, given by one Shepherd. And further, my son, be admonished by these. Of making many books there is no end, and much study is wearisome to the flesh.*
>
> *Let us hear the conclusion of the whole matter:*
> *Fear God and keep His commandments,*
> *For this is man's all.*
> *For God will bring every work into judgment,*
> *Including every secret thing,*
> *Whether good or evil.*
> *(Eccl. 12:8–14 NKJV)*

Theme: _____

Recommendation 1: _____

Recommendation 2: _____

To clarify the identity of the author, who is the "Preacher" mentioned in verses 8, 9, and 10?

What qualification does he claim to have (v. 9)? Do you agree with that assessment?

To what two things did he compare his own words (v. 11)?

To what two types of people did he compare himself (v. 11)?

What statement did he make that has probably been repeated by many students over the years, protesting their own homework (v. 12)?

Finally, do you agree with Solomon's concluding words in verse 14?

Pulling It All Together . . .

- Solomon begins this final section of Ecclesiastes with a call to enjoy life as much as we can, since death is on the way.

- He then cautions us to begin enjoying life as early as we can, for youth doesn't last long.

- He then cautions us to be as mature as possible, for bad decisions can come back to haunt us.

- He repeats his advice to make sure we enjoy life while we are young, because old age makes many enjoyments difficult or impossible.

- He ends by repeating his claim that most of life is foolishness, and he calls on his readers to fear God and keep His commandments—for *God knows and judges all.*

11

Coming to a Close

In mind In most of the study guides in this series, we have avoided referring to other authorities when it came time to summarize each book of the Bible. But Ecclesiastes is unique; as we said way back in the introduction, in the end it has to be read and considered as a complete unit rather than a series of chapters that can be read and understood separately.

To make things more complicated, sometimes Solomon seems to be speaking in a series of what linguists call *non sequiturs,* meaning that things don't always seem to follow logically from what went before. The truth is that Solomon was not being inconsistent or random, but even so, only by considering the whole thing at once can we really understand what he was saying.

Example 1—From an Ancient Viewpoint

With all the above in mind, let us look at three different ways to summarize the message of Ecclesiastes. The first example is based on the work of a man known in Jewish tradition by the acronym *RaMBaN*—or just Ramban. Ramban's full name and title was Rabbi Moses Ben Nachman (1194–1270). He lived most of his life in Spain but emigrated to Jerusalem near the end of his days. In his commentary on Ecclesiastes, written more than eight hundred years ago, he summed up what he considered its three main themes. These can be paraphrased as follows:

1. Solomon was a king of incredible wealth who knew what it meant to live a life of luxurious excess. From that experience Solomon learned firsthand that the pleasures and temptations of this world are fleeting at best, and utterly worthless at worst.

2. In contrast, our spirits are eternal, and therefore the spiritual relationships we establish with God during our brief lifetimes will endure forever. So we should willingly invest all the resources God gives us in serving Him as best we can, including our health, our wealth, and our time.

3. Even so, we still have to deal with the troubling questions of why good people often suffer and bad people often prosper (i.e., why bad things happen to good people and vice versa). But we cannot know the answers without knowing everything that God knows, including every single consideration, spanning throughout eternity, on which He bases each of His decisions. Since that kind of intelligence is far beyond our capacity, we cannot use what little we *do* understand as a basis for doubting God's justice. We cannot "make Him right or wrong" when we don't understand what He is doing. The kind of understanding we need will come to us only when the Messiah [whom Christians believe is Jesus Christ] comes and literally makes everything on earth as perfect as it was in the beginning. Until then we must act on faith and *trust God completely* in all things.

EXAMPLE 2—FROM AN ANALYTICAL VIEWPOINT

Another way of looking at the book of Ecclesiastes is to outline the entire text and see how it all shakes out. If we do that, we find that Solomon made three major points.

1. In verses 1:12 through 6:9, he said that most of what we do with our lives, *from an eternal perspective,* is essentially pointless. The chance that any of our accomplishments will last very long beyond us, if they even last throughout our earthly lifetimes, is very small. Likewise, the chance that we will ever be able to truly enjoy what we've accomplished here on earth is also pretty slim. Money and possessions do not guarantee happiness; neither do accolades and honors; neither does anything else we can pile up before we die.

2. In verses 6:10 through 11:6, he pointed out that we cannot possibly know which of our efforts will work out well and which will not. Because we are unable to see things from God's vantage point, we have no valid basis on which to establish any of our earthly priorities. Granted, any given effort might work out beautifully, but we cannot know that in advance.

3. In verses 11:7 through 12:14, Solomon brought Ecclesiastes to a close with an ultimate truth he mentioned once or twice before: the only way to guarantee a productive life is to live as righteously before God as we can. However, this will not necessarily yield what many of us might consider a happy or an easy life on earth. Rather, it will do something far more important—it will please God and bring us into eternal fellowship in His divine presence.

EXAMPLE 3—FROM A TEXTUAL VIEWPOINT

A third way of looking at Ecclesiastes uses the text itself to explain what Solomon meant to say. In the table below, the left-hand column lays out the basic principles that emerge from a careful reading, and the right-hand column illustrates each principle with verses from Ecclesiastes. Granted, this is not an exhaustive list, for we could put dozens of verses into the right-hand column. But this should give you a good picture of how Ecclesiastes delivers its message.

Principle	Reference from Ecclesiastes*
Happiness is a gift of God	Nothing is better for a man than that he should eat and drink, and that his soul should enjoy good in his labor. This also, I saw, was from the hand of God. *For who can eat, or who can have enjoyment, more than I?* For God gives wisdom and knowledge and joy to a man who is good in His sight; but to the sinner He gives the work of gathering and collecting, that he may give to him who is good before God. This also is vanity and grasping for the wind. (2:24–26, emphasis added)
	Every man should eat and drink and enjoy the good of all his labor—it is the gift of God. (3:13)
	As for every man to whom God has given riches and wealth, and given him power to eat of it, to receive his heritage and rejoice in his labor—this is the gift of God. For he will not dwell unduly on the days of his life, because God keeps him busy with the joy of his heart. (5:19–20)
	Go, eat your bread with joy, and drink your wine with a merry heart; for God has already accepted your works. (9:7)
that comes only to those who please Him,	For God gives wisdom and knowledge and joy to a man who is good in His sight; but to the sinner He gives the work of gathering and collecting, that he may give to him who is good before God. This also is vanity and grasping for the wind. (2:26)
fear Him,	Though a sinner does evil a hundred times, and his days are prolonged, yet I surely know that it will be well with those who fear God, who fear before Him. (8:12)
and recognize that He alone will judge them.	Rejoice, O young man, in your youth, and let your heart cheer you in the days of your youth; walk in the ways of your heart, and in the sight of your eyes; but know that for all these God will bring you into judgment. (11:9)

*All quotations in this table are taken from the New King James Version of the Bible.

ARE THERE ANY OTHER REASONS TO VALUE ECCLESIASTES?

Given the poetic language, the metaphoric approach, and what can often seem like a jaded, highly disillusioned, and even disdainful attitude toward humanity on Solomon's part, Ecclesiastes is not often considered an "easy read" for modern readers. But it still represents something unique in the Bible—a serious attempt, by the wisest man who ever lived, to prove through logic and observation alone that the smartest thing we can possibly do is what Solomon recommended in his last two verses:

> *Let us hear the conclusion of the whole matter:*
> *Fear God and keep His commandments,*
> *For this is man's all.*
> *For God will bring every work into judgment,*
> *Including every secret thing,*
> *Whether good or evil.*
> *(Eccl. 12:13–14)*

Fear God and keep His commandments. Notice that Solomon made no attempt whatsoever, anywhere in Ecclesiastes, to prove the existence of God. In his era, as pagan as many of his neighbors were, the existence of the one true God of the universe, who created everything and yet desires above all else to be in close, intimate, eternal fellowship with us, was simply not in doubt.

Sadly, in the modern era, God's existence seems to be undecided in the minds of many. But in the long run, humankind's desperate attempts to discredit God amount to nothing more than one more external distraction from what we believers should be concentrating on.

Fearing God, keeping His commandments, and thus doing our part to maintain a close, personal, intimate relationship with him. Nothing else matters more, now and forever.

And no body of truth, gathered from anywhere in the universe, could possibly have more eternal value than the wondrous gift Solomon has given us in the book of Ecclesiastes.

HOW TO BUILD YOUR REFERENCE LIBRARY

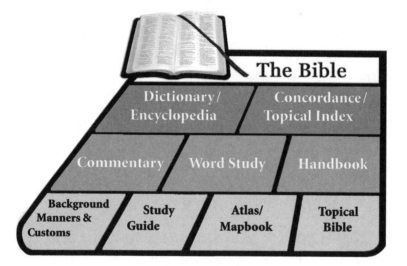

GREAT RESOURCES FOR BUILDING YOUR REFERENCE LIBRARY

DICTIONARIES AND ENCYCLOPEDIAS

All About the Bible: The Ultimate A-to-Z® Illustrated Guide to the Key People, Places, and Things

Every Man in the Bible by Larry Richards

Every Woman in the Bible by Larry Richards and Sue Richards

Nelson's Compact Bible Dictionary

Nelson's Illustrated Encyclopedia of the Bible

Nelson's New Illustrated Bible Dictionary

Nelson's Student Bible Dictionary

So That's What It Means! The Ultimate A-to-Z Resource by Don Campbell, Wendell Johnston, John Walvoord, and John Witmer

Vine's Complete Expository Dictionary of Old and New Testament Words by W. E. Vine and Merrill F. Unger

CONCORDANCES AND TOPICAL INDEXES

Nelson's Quick Reference Bible Concordance by Ronald F. Youngblood

The New Strong's Exhaustive Concordance of the Bible by James Strong

COMMENTARIES

Believer's Bible Commentary by William MacDonald

Matthew Henry's Concise Commentary on the Whole Bible by Matthew Henry

The MacArthur Bible Commentary by John MacArthur

Nelson's New Illustrated Bible Commentary

Thru the Bible series by J. Vernon McGee

HANDBOOKS

Nelson's Compact Bible Handbook

Nelson's Complete Book of Bible Maps and Charts

Nelson's Illustrated Bible Handbook

Nelson's New Illustrated Bible Manners and Customs by Howard F. Vos

With the Word: The Chapter-by-Chapter Bible Handbook by Warren W. Wiersbe

For more great resources, please visit *www.thomasnelson.com.*

NELSON IMPACT BIBLE STUDY GUIDE SERIES

Written in an easy-to-read, interesting style, these study guides will help you to experience the true meaning of the messages of the Bible, and in turn, empower you to truly make a difference in the world for Christ.

Available at your local Christian Bookstore

NELSON IMPACT
A Division of Thomas Nelson Publishers
Since 1798

www.thomasnelson.com

The Finest Study Bible EVER!

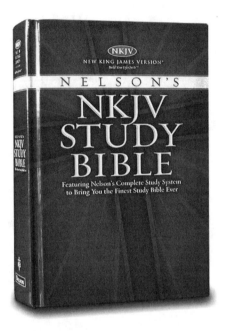

Nelson's NKJV Study Bible helps you understand, apply and grow in a life-long journey through God's Word.

NEW KING JAMES VERSION®
Build Your Life On It™

NELSON IMPACT
A Division of Thomas Nelson Publishers
Since 1798

The Nelson Impact Team is here to answer your questions and suggestions as to how we can create more resources that benefit you, your family, and your community.

Contact us at Impact@thomasnelson.com